Writing   s

Writing a Thriller

THIRD EDITION

André Jute

A & C Black • London

Third edition 1999
First published 1986
Second edition 1994

A & C Black (Publishers) Limited
35 Bedford Row, London WC1R 4JH

© 1999, 1986, 1994, André Jute

ISBN 0–7136–5093–1

A CIP catalogue record for this book
is available from the British Library.

Typeset in 10½ on 12½ pt Sabon
Printed and bound in Great Britain by
Creative Print and Design (Wales), Ebbw Vale

Contents

For my Mother,
who made all things possible

1. How to Use this Book

In this book I intend to provide you with 0.9% of the fabric that makes up a published writer; that is the most help anyone can realistically offer the aspiring writer. The rest of the whole writer is made up of 0.1% communicative ability, often miscalled 'talent' – and the remaining 99.0% is 'perseverance', which aptly describes the writer's condition. The 0.9% I'm offering help with is the nitty-gritty of craft and technique without which no-one, no matter how talented or keen, can write a novel, of which the thriller is a sub-genre.

First, let's answer an important question:

can *you* write a thriller?

Yes, almost certainly you can write a thriller. The fact that you are often in a bookstore or a library and therefore presumably a reader is all the evidence required. I shall enlarge on this in a moment, but right now we can sound an additional encouraging note: you have a book about writing in your hand, so obviously *you* have some kind of a hankering to write and at least a small spark of confidence that you may be able to do so. These are steps of vastly greater importance than may appear at present. Whether you *will* write the novel you are capable of is another matter.

This book is aimed at the aspiring writer who wants to make a career or profession of writing, to have his or her book (from now on his includes her, but don't forget there are more female fiction writers than male) published and to write more books for publication.

Communication skills

There is no innate skill in communication that fiction writers have and you don't. That many, at this stage probably most, of

1

them are better *storytellers* than you is not a matter of their good fortune but of their application to their craft, and of long apprenticeships in order to acquire or invent the techniques of their success.

The writer's tools and techniques

The writer's tools are:

- the language – which he acquired by osmosis just as you did – developed to a greater or lesser pitch;
- his senses – which you also share – guided by experience and practice in gathering and filtering what is useful to him as a writer;
- a number of techniques (and even tricks) of the trade – which he learned by observation, study and trial-and-error practice – to which this book offers a shortcut, though you will still have to practise, and
- an indomitable will.

This last is a tool so important we will discuss it below under its own heading, 'Perseverance'.

Your use of language is of course important and I shall have much to say about the purpose and effect of language, but you will shortly notice that there is no section headed 'Language, the use of'. This is for the good reason that no-one can presume to teach you the 'proper' use of language for your own fiction. Any such attempt may actually detract from the unique freshness of your expression. You acquire skill in expression as you practise on your keyboard, as a subsumed function of characterization and narrative.

As for observation, it is akin to use of language and far more personal to each individual writer. In preparation for this book, I attended a class for would-be writers run by a lady who shall remain nameless; I used only the first part of my double-barrelled name, the part that doesn't appear on my books. She took us on a nature walk through lanes I have long loved, then set us an essay about our walk. Later I was publicly berated for having 'seen nothing, smelt nothing, heard nothing of glorious Mother Nature'; my piece dealt with what the other people on the trek had said and done. Detailed descriptions of things and places aren't my style; dialogue and action are. Out of curiosity, I borrowed one of this lady's books from the library and, truly, her descriptions, ream upon ream, are luminous but – dare I say? – a mite boring after the first fifty pages. From what I've seen of her students' work, they've turned into pale carbon copies.

Every writer will observe what is useful to him as a writer; don't let anyone force a straitjacket on your eyes and ears. What you see, and how you see it, is as much part of your originality as uniquely expressive language. In reading John Braine's book on J. B. Priestley, I was struck by Braine's glee (there really is no more apt word for his emotion) at realizing that Priestley saw many things the same way he did. The same great joy in recognizing a kindred spirit shines through the essays on other writers by the novelist John Wain. In both cases there is an implicit admission by these men as *novelists* that sometimes they have felt their creative vision to be out of step but now recognize it as part of what made them, and other men, good writers. 'Observation' is not something you work at consciously – in fact, I never knew what manner of observation was *my* kind until critics told me what they had read into my books. The nearest you will come to understanding, until you receive feedback from your own published books, is when you read someone's book and you exclaim, 'My god, he sees it, I see it, why doesn't everyone see it?'

What does that leave about which I may presume to instruct you? Imagine for a moment that I am a master cabinet maker and you are my apprentice. Our exchanges and demonstrations would ignore the 'art' of Chippendale and concentrate exclusively and exhaustively on the marking-out of dovetail joints, the laying on of veneers, the gluing and clamping of joints, the parts that together make up the outer form 'Chippendale', the very selection, cutting and drying of the wood that will go into the furniture you plan to build. I really do urge you to think of this book, and the task of becoming a published writer, in exactly that way. The cabinet maker had to master all the skills before he could design and build fine furniture with those flourishes of his own that distinguish the master from the journeyman. You have an advantage: *he* had first to learn to use his tools by practising on small offcuts, whereas your tools – character and plot – become the end product almost as soon as you create them and you work on the whole suite of furniture from the very beginning.

Perseverance

A Nobel laureate told me that, within a six-block radius of the bar we were in, there were a hundred better writers than either of us – very decent of him to include me. The difference between us, as published writers, and them, as unpublished writers (perhaps not even knowing what fame they could be missing), was merely that we sat down and wrote a page every day or ten pages every day or some other immutable number, and didn't stop until we had that number – and they didn't. This didn't shock me as much as the rest of the company, because I already knew from experience in advertising, motor racing and film making that the difference between the leading practitioner and a mere journeyman lies mostly in the application each brings to his craft.

Some years later I was reminded of this when the chief editor of a big New York publisher came to see me in Cambridge (England) where I then lived and, meeting me for the first time after travelling three thousand miles, straight off the train started questioning me intensively about my health, the sports I took part in, my attitude to diet and exercise – a shockingly discourteous performance. Later I would discover that he correlates an author's health with his ability to take the knocks, do the rewrites, get another book out. In other words, perseverance. The world's top literary agent calls it 'stickitivity' and, incidentally, rates it at 99.9%. Novelist Andrew McCoy has a reader's report which says, 'I hate this novel but, after seeing several of this author's manuscripts, I am convinced he will carry on and eventually be published. Perhaps you should have a chat with him. Recommend rejection.' The novel the reader hated was *Atrocity Week*, which was published by another house (on the recommendation of the first publisher after the 'chat') and became a bestseller. A famous publisher once said, 'Don't bring me any first novels, bring me eighth novels.' Make your own list of now famous novels that were turned down x number of times before some smart publisher hit the jackpot;

4

my own *Reverse Negative* was rewritten forty-three times and turned down by forty-four publishers, including, the first time I offered it, by two of the three houses who later published it simultaneously in New York, London and Australia. It won me international acclaim, the ego trip of translations and book club choices, and made enough money to launch my career, yet I have quite a few letters damning it as 'unpublishable'. Meanwhile, I had honed my skills on that novel over a period of two to three years, while at the same time creating the novel itself, surely something of value.

The point of these anecdotes is that all these eminent people, and I, are calling the same thing by different names. It is rare to find everyone involved in the making of a book in agreement, but the one thing that unites us all is this faith in perseverance. Specifically, perseverance is that 99.0% of blood, sweat, toil and tears that you put in to turn your god-given 0.1% of communicative skill – plus the 0.9% of craft you can learn from me or by trial and error – into a publishable novel. In automobile design they have a word: iteration. It means doing it over – and over and over and over – until you get it right. Only you can do it.

The writer's greatest virtue is never to give up. If you were born stubborn, obstinate and plain pig-headed, you have a good start.

On bibliographies and exercises

Originally I intended to include a bibliography of other 'how to' texts for the aspiring author. After finishing the first draft of this book, I read as many as I could lay my hands on. I had not read any before, having taught myself to write by trial and error at my typewriter with a lot of help from my friends. After reading them, I decided to dispense with the bibliography and recommend to you with all my heart only one other instructional text, John Braine's *Writing a Novel**. Mr Braine is a 'straight' novelist and a thriller writer of note and it is clear that he knows what he is talking about. His advice also differs from that offered in these pages often and substantially enough

---

*Presently out of print but available second-hand and on inter-library loan

to make it worth your while reading his book (aside from the pure pleasure of his prose, but that you can find in his novels, too) as well as this one. A thriller writer needs no larger shopping list than his book and this one. I'm sorry if this sounds arrogant, and Mr Braine will probably horsewhip me for daring to rank my book just below his, but some of the advice in several of the available texts would, if I had taken it as a novice, have ensured that I remained unpublished. I must assume it could do you the same harm. The laws of libel prevent me from particularizing further but, if you browse among texts for writers, sieve the advice you receive through a very fine mesh of incredulity. That applies to this book too. Try anything, but accept only what works for you.

In fairness, you should know that I am the author of three further books for other writers (rather than for thriller writers in particular) in the fields I practise in myself. They are *Start Writing Today!*, *Keep on Writing!* and *Writing Proposals & Synopses that Sell*. The first two take the writer of creative fiction and non-fiction from amateur beginnings to earning a living as a professional writer, the third is a tool for writers to ensure their ideas receive a fair hearing in the modern, typically conglomerate, publishing house.

There are very few exercises in this book for you to do. Simple exercises are a waste of time and an insult; difficult exercises require personal guidance to get the most from them. The one major exercise, aimed at helping writers with a very specific and unfortunately common need, is in an appendix. Examples, too, are not plentiful because I assume you read widely and will find your own examples to suit your needs and style; many examples are taken from genres other than thrillers, not only because it is increasingly difficult to draw the line between thrillers and 'novels of suspense', but because the general (as opposed to detective) thriller became respectable enough to attract good and even outstanding writers only a single generation ago, say, since Condon's *The Manchurian Candidate*.

In addition to examples from, or references to, general literature, you will find I lay considerable emphasis on imports from other media. Readers are exposed to real world influences that daily make new entries in their lexicon of ideas; the professional writer must compete with a babel of voices. Methods, means and attitudes imported from other media can, of course, be a boon to the open-minded writer.

For veterans only

Chapter 6 definitely carries a health warning for new writers. The matters considered in that chapter actively encourage you to breach several of the proven practices on which the true beginner's successful use of this book depends.

A mechanical example is that the section on the way characters in different ages are *born* different generally (but not exclusively) applies to concepts which play out over longer than the twelve-month narrative period that novices can handle without losing themselves in complexities.

Chapter 6 also includes a section on advanced plotting structures which will be of more use to writers with the confidence of considerable practice in the easier methods of Chapter 5.

If you are a novice, you are therefore advised to skip Chapter 6 until you are confident in your command of a writer's proven tools, say, until you have a book at the publisher's, one in the drawer awaiting a final polish, another on the screen, and start casting around for ideas for your fourth book.

Other advanced ideas are scattered throughout the text but, wherever possible, there is a clear progression to them and multiple choices for writers at all levels of skill.

When you can stop using this book

Throughout I shall assume that you are writing or planning a thriller of substantial length – a novella can be as few as 40,000 words, a novel a minimum of 60,000 words. 80,000 are considered more respectable and at present the favoured length is generally about 80,000–100,000 words. What I suggest is that you read this book from cover to cover and then refer back to the relevant chapters at various stages during your own work.

A word of caution: the advice in this book works for me and has been observed, also by me, to work for other writers. The test is not academic dogma or fine-sounding theories but efficacy in practice. However, despite obvious general application, it is still personal opinion, not wisdom graven on stone tablets. You should be able to measure your progress by the rate at which you adapt the advice in this book to your own requirements, skills and experience. If, in preparing for your third or fourth or fifth novel, you were to read this text and find that half of it is old hat because it has become second nature to you and the other half irrelevant because you've adapted it to yourself to such an extent that it is quite unrecognizable – then I shall be very happy, because this book will be a success.

2. Why Write Thrillers?

I confess, I'm a voracious thriller reader. I read good thrillers and bad thrillers, any thrillers I find on the shelves of my library. I also read a great deal of non-fiction and biography and technical books and good 'straight' modern novels when I can find them – which is not often, so that I'm continually cast back on the classics.

What do *you* read by habit?

Make a list of what you read. You will be surprised at how catholic your reading is. Now, make a list of what you *don't* read. It should be obvious from your list that, if you have no taste for historical romances, it is not likely that you will be able to write one with conviction and passion, even if your bank manager keeps telling you the world's bestselling novelist is Catherine Cookson. Again, unless you can read the Mills & Boon type of love story without disdain and preferably with real enjoyment, readers of your own attempt at the genre will promptly spot that your heart isn't in it.

Your bookshelves will tell a keen observer who you are and, more importantly, what your aspirations are.

If you are a cosmopolitan without any empathy for the naïve Catherine Cookson type of character, you will never be able to write such characters convincingly. As a young, hungry writer, I read a few Mills & Boon and similar novels; I marvelled at the skill and control of their construction – and I despised the waste of talent on such trivial material for such an audience. Today I am much more tolerant, and grateful that a wise old agent, agreeing that I had the pasticheur's talent to write a passable *faux* Mills & Boon novel, told me not to do it. As an aside, I now know that I don't possess the control to do a thing so much against my nature. But the beginning writer by definition lacks the experience which brings such self-knowledge.

It is much safer to write what you like to read and admire rather than what you think will sell.

Why write *thrillers*?

All the same, having excluded the books you don't read, you will still be left with a substantial list of those you can really put your heart into, one class of which will, if you are a thriller reader, probably be thrillers. How to choose?

Many writers will tell you, 'I never made a conscious choice. I started writing what I like to read because I'd run through all the good books at the library.' Or, 'I just had to write that.' Probably true; I do not remember making a conscious choice, merely following a path of least resistance and greatest enjoyment.

There is no such thing as pure entertainment but the thriller is a taste and a field so catholic and fertile that something pretty near pure entertainment can grow at one end while, at the other, one finds important novels of deep thought and commitment. You should, I think, choose your position in this spectrum according to what you like reading.

If you enjoy John Grisham's books, don't try for the Graham Greene touch merely because you think it is more 'respectable' or sells better. From the writer the same level of skill is required but for the reader what matters is where your heart is.

There are a number of negative reasons for choosing not to write thrillers:

- the pace requirement is more strenuous than in any other kind of fiction except the adventure story;
- the writer has less breathing space to establish and build convincing characters and the skills required here, too, are therefore higher;
- the top-level competition is ruthlessly professional and invidious comparisons with other thrillers by critics are far more likely than in the case of the straight novel;
- readers have been conditioned to such a degree of realism that any new writer's research must be impeccable if he is not to be laughed out of court.

This is an awesome list of obstacles but equally formidable, if different, hurdles face the aspirant writer in other genres and the would-be professional in any field of worthwhile endeavour.

In the chapters to follow, you and I will deal methodically with the obstacles. First, positive motivations for choosing to write thrillers:

- there is a very extensive market; check library and bookstore paperback shelves and you will find a large supply of thrillers to satisfy an equally large demand;

- within this large market there is a demand for thrillers at all levels, from the crudest booze-battles-broads private eye to the sophisticated, subtle thriller which is indistinguishable from the novel of literary merit;

- while there is space for the talented beginner, improvement in skill is recognized, encouraged and rewarded;

- there is a high standard of published writing to study and emulate;

- the sub-classes and types of thriller are many and it is easy for the writer established in one type to gain access to others (whereas it is difficult, for instance, for a writer of family sagas to be accepted as anything else);

- thrillers have good subsidiary aftermarkets in book club, paperback and film sales. (This is a very important source of income for the professional writer, because libraries buy at most a few thousand hardcover copies and private individuals almost none except through book clubs; I have made more money merely out of *options* for film on my books than I have ever made from hardcover sales; even a book sold cheaply for film will earn as much as book royalties on five or six bestsellers. This is not an argument for writing directly for films: you'll never get through the front door.)

- the thriller is now a respectable genre, if such things are important to you. (The better thrillers are reviewed respectfully in all the best places; a moment's thought will persuade you that the same is not true of almost all the other types of genre fiction. There was a time when the likes of Queenie Leavis could sneer at thrillers as somehow *infra dig* but in the intervening three quarters of a century the thriller has become the preferred reading and, in many cases, the chosen form of self-expression of the intellectual élite. Who's afraid of Queenie Leavis?)

What *makes* a thriller?

A thriller is defined as a narrative wherein the reader experiences a vicarious thrill by identifying with both the deeds of high daring performed by the hero and the dangers to which he is exposed. Exotic places and people are optional – and the thriller can be as intellectually challenging as the writer chooses to make it or the reader elects to find it.

The modern thriller shares a common origin with the adventure story. The roots of both can be traced to the ancient epic poems but that's mainly of interest to scholars. For practical purposes, Edgar Allan Poe, H. Rider Haggard, Arthur Conan Doyle and John Buchan are the grandfathers of the modern mainstream thriller in form, content, language and virtually every other dimension. Scholarly and popular texts available at your library trace the influence of these and other writers of that generation on the thriller in general and various minority groupings within it, but you can learn all that much more enjoyably by reading Haggard, Conan Doyle, Buchan and Poe themselves. I mention this, not because it is essential to your art, but because your enjoyment of your work will be enhanced if you are aware of its roots – and also so that you do not rediscover the wheel!

The techniques of writing adventure stories and thrillers are similar, though the *depth* of application of each technique differs. Where the modern thriller (in its narrowest definition) parts company with the modern adventure story is in sophistication of motive and action; thus the thriller has almost always a betrayal *from within*, whereas the adventure story almost always tells in a more straightforward way of achieving a goal against *outside* resistance. Of course this is an over-simplification but at least one paperback publisher finds it invaluable for labelling books 'adventure' or 'thriller'. However, unless there are other and compelling reasons such as that you *prefer* adventure novels, do not let the greater sophistication required in handling the layers of guilt and betrayal in a thriller direct you to writing an adventure instead. Not only do adventures almost inevitably require exotic settings and knowledge – I cringe every time I read certain authors who obviously have never set foot in Africa – but they also demand great skill in keeping the action moving unflaggingly at a much greater pace than is normally necessary in a thriller.

What differentiates the thriller and adventure story from all other literary forms is a greater serving of tension. All narratives depend to some extent on tension – you would not continue reading if you did not want to know what happens next – but in the thriller and adventure tension is the definitive ingredient. We shall spend much time and effort in the chapters following on the techniques of creating tension, and of highlighting tension where it is inherent in characters and situations.

In this book, 'thriller' is used to include 'adventure' unless otherwise specified.

What is a thriller?

This is a trick question. Certainly 'a thriller' is fiction rather than non-fiction, but that still leaves a very wide field. Nor will it do to exclude certain classes of fiction, such as historical novels. John Webbe, in a review of my novel *The Zaharoff Commission*, seems to find genre distinctions, even that between fiction and non-fiction, unwieldy: 'Jute joins a select few historians of the more serious order in crediting Zaharoff with the diplomatic coup that stopped World War I. The story unfolds and races along into a succession of intriguing and often bizarre events with the speed of any thriller hard to put down. But the element of historical fact claims for it a place among some of the better works, in all their forms, to which this war gave rise.'* Webbe's was the only notice to use the word 'thriller' for a novel that was widely reviewed as a useful contribution to historical research and interpretation; two of my publishers labelled it merely 'a novel'. Yet there is no doubt that it is a thriller: the subject matter is a spying mission the armaments dealer Basil Zaharoff undertook behind the German lines in July 1918 to bring back information which the Premier of France was convinced ended the First World War.

Making a list of thriller types is also undesirable but it is the least evil. Remember, this is *my* list – yours could be different.

The Advertiser, Adelaide

The world of the spy thriller-writer

Percentages

Writers are more realistic in presentation of:
international issues, motivation & behaviour of spies	90
social conditions, technology of espionage, politicians who in theory control services	80

Spy novels now glamorize spies less
	95
are less nationalistic	90
more critical of secret activities	90
more concerned morally	75

Should writer try to influence readers?
No	65
Yes	30
Story/characters will influence them	5

Are you influenced by critics?
Yes	50
No	40
Don't know (and other)	10

Plots & characters come mainly from
life	40
imagination	20
both	40

Most entertaining spy novel you have read:
Spy Who Came in from the Cold	30
Tinker, Tailor, Soldier, Spy	15
From Russia with Love	10

Most influential spy novel since 1945
Spy Who Came in from the Cold	60

Most important before 1945
The Thirty-nine Steps	30
Eric Ambler's novels	30

To discover a man's self-image, ask him what he thinks of his peers. Miss Helen Valls-Russell of the University of Perpignan collected these opinions from published cloak-and-dagger authors for a post-graduate study of spy fiction, but they speak equally eloquently about spy-fiction writers. I'm indebted to another member of this talented family, the journalist and occasional thriller writer (*The Beirut Pipeline*) Mr Laurie Valls-Russell, for defining a good thriller as one so well written that it may be reread for pleasure after the dénouement is known.

The whodunnit

This is the classic type of thriller, the locked room mystery, and, if one is an aficionado, surprisingly easy to perpetrate even for the ten-thumbed. There is a big market and the sub-genre has been respectable for a century now; you'll be in good company. The main trick is to find new characters and environments. At the turn of the millennium, it seems to me that the religious and their environment have had a big boost from Umberto Eco's mainstream novel *The Name of the Rose* a quarter of a century ago and the well-deserved success of Ellis Peters's Father Cadfael.

The police procedural

This is an outgrowth of the detective novel and, since it must offer realistic police procedures, requires specific knowledge of how the police force depicted operates; many police forces are only too happy to help, especially if you ask specific rather than general questions to prove you've done your homework. You don't have to stick to Scotland Yard and New York's finest either – Amsterdam and Paris and Bombay have equally fine fictional cops and other places have as yet unsung heroes. This sub-genre, which often makes a social point, requires more skill in characterization than whodunnits.

The caper

The 'crime procedural' equivalent on the other side of the law. Unless you're a professional journalist with crime-reporting experience, do your research in the library – criminals are paranoid and violent people who are not likely to see any humour in a request for their organization chart, and private enterprise security firms under scrutiny also have a tendency to violence. On the other hand, you have a distinct choice between a serious treatment tending to a straight novel about the criminal mentality (*The Godfather*) and the light touch or near-send-up (*Topkapi, Only When I Larf, The Hot Rock*) in which you can really let your imagination rip as long as you get your machine detail right – see Chapter 7 on research.

Private eyes

These range from the booze/battles/broads masturbatory aids of Carter Brown to the subtle and impeccably crafted novels of

Victor Canning and Ross Macdonald. The spectrum also includes variations on the theme, for instance Oliver Bleeck/ Ross Thomas's go-between, who ransoms stolen goods/people from thieves for the insurance companies. 'If you're a feminist,' says one New York publisher, 'you should seriously consider creating a female private eye.' Her even harder-boiled London counterpart says tartly, 'Even if you're just a woman, it will be good for your bank balance.' Books in this sub-genre have an excellent aftermarket in paperback and especially in television and films.

Spies

The archetypal thriller of the twentieth century, though the form is as old as wandering epic singers (who were themselves often spies). The main requirement is specific knowledge of how security services operate but that is easy to come by: the security services of two nations confiscated the manuscripts of *Reverse Negative* because they thought I knew too much and was pointing fingers, yet every single fact in it had come from the books on the shelves of the South Australian State Library and all the conclusions followed logically from the correct juxtaposition and interpretation of the facts. Anthony Blunt's exposure followed immediately on publication. However, this is a tricky sub-genre, as Cold War books have become a bit of a glut with publishers. Spies are not dead though; they have merely found other targets (drug dealers among others) and ways of surviving (entering crime themselves). You might also consider that, though it was not often mentioned, much spying carried on by the official spies was not military but commercial and industrial. In the communications age we have already entered, such skills take on special importance.

The political thriller

In the USA, this sub-genre could be sub-titled 'Armageddon in Washington', in Britain, 'Choirboys in Cabinet Beds'. These are tales of high-level brinkmanship illuminated for the reader by portraits of those in high places, often thinly disguised photographs of real men in power. Again, the special knowledge of the inner workings of government is available at your local library.

Fashionable losers
This is a version of the spy thriller or the political thriller where the central character is not a top person or one who lives dangerously but one of life's fashionable losers, say a journalist, dragged into dangerous doings against his will by those fatal accidents of the secret state/multi-national finance/crazed power bosses/plain horse thieves, this last a Dick Francis speciality. A variation is the boy or the girl next door – say, an accountant, with whom middle-class folk can easily identify – dropped in the deep end by those fatal accidents of the secret state, etc.

The psychological thriller
This is essentially a straight novel about everyday or exceptional people who lead normal lives until... The important point is that the outside influence, normally an evil person, must be built up quite slowly so that the dénouement comes as a shock to the characters as well as to the reader. This is very tricky to achieve and successes on library shelves are few and far between. A knowledge of motivational, abnormal and perhaps para-psychology, though not essential, would come in useful for the aspirant writer in this branch of the thriller.

The chiller
This is a less sophisticated psychological thriller, usually relying on supernatural events for its tension. It is a bastard by Edgar Allan Poe out of Emily Brontë and is rightfully a gothic sub-genre but the requirement for high tension demands that it be created with thriller writing techniques rather than high-romance skills (where they differ, which is less often than might at first meet the eye). There's a huge market for these books and, if you read and enjoy them, probably a place in the sun for you, too. I sometimes get the feeling that any knowledge of para-psychology would damage the unfettered imagination of the established writers in this field – but that may just be envy of the way the shekels roll in to them!

The return of the Apocalypse – Doomsday strikes Metropolis
The disaster novel, too, is a thriller sub-genre. The previous edition of this book (1994) stated: 'I have no hesitation in fore-casting that the wheel will roll and the disaster film will come

back as a big moneyspinner; meanwhile disaster novels of originality do well in hardcover and reasonably in paperback.' It happened; the disaster is a perennial; its success depends on presentation. There is much to recommend this form to the new thriller writer: purpose-directed research is always easier than looking for something you'll know when you see it, the potential disaster almost creates its own characters, conflict and tension are built in, the pace is inherent, there is a great big chunky climax waiting for you right from the beginning of the book. In addition, the disaster novel seems now to have become respectable – my *Sinkhole* was reviewed at substantial length in *The Times Literary Supplement*.

The adventure story
Adventures, too, are thrillers, distinguished only by more straightforward narrative and motivation. This is a huge market and, it seems to me, one generally much more sparsely populated with writers than the rest of the thriller domain, which implies that individual writers sell a lot of books. Wilbur Smith paperback impressions of a million copies are common gossip in the trade… But, as pointed out above, a very high level of skill is required to pace an adventure novel correctly, which perhaps explains why there are not more adventure writers.

Lawyers…
Right now, 1999, every publisher whose antennae aren't terminally worn is beating the bushes for a lawyer who can write a thriller, or any writer who can write a thriller about a lawyer. There is also a richly rewarding sub-branch in pathologists and other such law enforcement ancillaries.

…and medicos…
The standard medical thriller continues to attract readers. Do not be put off by the technical expertise required. It is as near as your family doctor or your nearest library.

…and stockbrokers
A huge, virtually unexplored field, one in which the necessary expertise is almost ridiculously easy to acquire and the plots can be read in the pink pages daily.

You will of course think of many other classes of thrillers but these main headings give an idea of the scope to which the techniques outlined in this book are applicable. Many of the techniques can obviously be used in any kind of narrative but those particular to or more heavily called upon in the writing of a thriller are correspondingly more emphatically treated.

Hot/Not

Kenneth Atchity of the AEI literary agency in Los Angeles publishes a 'Hot/Not' list. He was once a professor of literature but he came into the business through being a film and television producer, which he still is. His list of what the movies want and hate *right now* is therefore influenced by his environment and experience. What is hot and what is not hot in Hollywood changes so often that Atchity is forced to maintain his list on the Internet, where he can update it once every week or ten days. I shall not reproduce his list here, because, before I finish rewriting the next chapter, it will be outdated.

However, it is striking that Atchity's 'yes, please!' list is almost word for word the same recommendations as are dotted throughout this book – and have been ever since its first edition fourteen years ago, though Atchity gets round to insisting that thrillers must be 'intelligent' even more hastily than I do; the situation has changed so that at the very bottom the market doesn't just have less space, the space has disappeared, a subject we shall touch on again.

Even more striking is Atchity's 'no, never, bugger-off' list: he says the movies don't want any sports books, which is precisely what I told you fourteen years ago in the first edition of this book. Among the other things the movies don't want are a few fleeting fashions, but in the main we can conclude that film producers *do* want to buy books about interesting characters doing interesting things.

Atchity is said by his detractors to be 'too big on the story'. The mind boggles.

Now, I'm not telling you this because I have stars in my eyes. Quite the contrary. I'm of the Len Deighton school: take the film producer's money and run before he can waste years of your life. But the film distributors and financiers are now so tied up with the book publishers that Atchity, who routinely offers the book for film rights before he even shows it to a publisher, could be the leading edge of the next generation of agents.

This, if it turns out to be a universal trend, could have serious consequences for artists who work in a field where the primary and only financially viable form, a full-length novel, can take anything from three months to a year or more to complete. We shall have to see whether it matters to most writers, or just a few stars. Personally, I don't care or bother with this week's fashion in Los Angeles. For instance, I have just finished writing a book set against the background of motor racing. One or more publishers will want it: grand prix racing is now, next to soccer, the biggest live attendance and television viewership sport in the world. Motor racing is also the sport of the middle classes, the same people who buy books. And I wanted to write it, which is a more than adequate reason.

But note the description: 'against the background of motor racing' – *not* 'a motor racing book'. My focus is on people, not technology. We shall return again and again to the focus on character, because it makes any genre, niche or subject fresh, regardless of what is fashionable when at last you finish your book.

Spies, in our list above, are out of fashion this week. But, ask yourself, what do spies do when there is no spying to be done because their masters have carelessly made peace? If they have any brains, they talk themselves into a job fighting drugs criminals, as Britain's MI5 (the Security Service or counter-intelligence agency) have done.

And isn't what a spy, out of a job and out of fashion, will do with his special and especially underhand skills in desperation to put bread on the table for his family a seriously interesting subject?

Make your own list, and then consider whether, under strong attack by someone of the calibre of Kenneth Atchity, you would be able to defend your list because it is what you truly want to read, therefore what you truly want to write, consequently what you can truly write well.

What people like you want to read, what you want to write, what you can write well – is what will sell. Not the other way round.

3. Genius, Osmosis or Theft: finding your plot and characters

One day your novel will spring fully fledged to mind. That day you will know you could be a novelist. Some years and several completed novels later, you will be able immediately to start writing and to finish the novel as you conceived it. That day you will be a time-served fully professional novelist. In between lies the dangerous period when most aspiring writers give up, because they find, when they sit down to write the novel so clear in their minds in that first moment of insight, that the shape is too large to form whole on the page and they lack the skill to put it down piecemeal. Unfortunately, there is no other way to write a novel *but* piecemeal and it is here, in helping you find the tools to chop your flash of genius into manageable mouthfuls, that this book should earn its keep.

There is an alternative problem, which afflicts the writer starting a second or subsequent novel more often than the complete novice: you want to write a book but you have no idea about what. This is another professional hurdle: if you don't vault it you will never be a professional writer, who is defined as someone who *writes regularly*. The luxury of awaiting inspiration is enjoyed solely by amateurs. If you want to be a professional, you cannot tarry until someday you fortuitously happen upon 'something to say', you must search for and find a theme and characters to write about. Search long enough and a moment of stillness (John Braine's telling phrase) will overcome you, the concept will flood in and you will once more be in the frame of mind of the newborn novelist described above. If you are not religious, this is the nearest to resurrection you will ever come.

But, while the experience is easily described in semi-mystic terms, it is won by hard graft at the technicalities of our craft. Mastery of the tools of the trade helps you finish any novel you

21

start (if you don't, you may never start another) and further ensures that you always *will* have a novel to start.

The writer's origination tools

These tools are used in exactly the same way whether you wish to dissect an apparently fully fledged idea into manageable portions or to generate the foundation of a novel where you may be starting with a blank mind. They are, in order of formalization:

The concept or theme or idea

This is that flash of genius in which the novel seems completely realized but when written down may well be a single sentence: 'Woman married to brutal husband falls in love with elegant ghost from different period who haunts their beautiful house.' Or my note for *The Zaharoff Commission*: 'Zaharoff's mission to Germany in July 1918 at the behest of Lloyd George and Clemenceau to find out how near Communists were to taking over Berlin and declaring unilateral ceasefire before War could be ended by military means – see Donald McCormick's standard biography of Zaharoff, *Pedlar of Death*.' Or this: 'What if the Mafia were to corner the silver market? (All other precious metals too big or widely held.)' which I filed in the wastepaper basket the day after Paul Erdman's *The Silver Bears* appeared. We shall shortly return to these ideas, their sources and recognition.

Characters

These are the people who will by their actions illustrate your concept or idea. For the professional novelist it is axiomatic that plot flows from character. This is such an important principle that in several of the following chapters I shall point up commercial and artistic reasons for this belief. The writer who lacks a concept for his next book also looks to what *people* do to find one – people at work, people on the block or at the club, people in the news or on the shelves at his library. Once you have your concept, you usually have at least some of the characters, because they are the ones whose actions, real and observable or merely likely and conjured up in your imagination, suggested the concept to you. Essentially, you find your characters the way you find your concepts; the difficult part lies in fleshing them out from those insightful flashes you have about them. We shall devote the whole of the next chapter to the creation of your characters.

Character-generated plot

These are the actions that the characters undertake because of the relationships they have and the frictions inherent in such contact. In a sense, if you create your characters right, you don't use this tool, it uses you by acting as a control on the rest of your work – if nothing sparks between your characters, you must either create new characters or you won't have a publishable novel. This, too, is described in detail in the next chapter.

The detailed plot

This is a means of constructing a chronological and consequential outline which traces your concept through the actions of your characters; the resulting outline is most conveniently understood as a schedule of motivations for their essential actions. We shall return to the detailed plot in Chapter 5.

The concept: sources and recognition

Recognition is a tautological process: if you recognize an idea or concept as the backbone of a novel, it is right for you. Professional novelists and first-timers alike tell one: 'I just had to write it.' If you don't accept the potential of an idea emotionally as well as rationally it will do you no good, no matter how plausible it may be in the hands of another writer.

Many writers will also tell you, 'I took it from real life, old boy,' but that's a defence mechanism – they may fear that too close an inspection of the manner in which their plots come to them may destroy the delicate subconscious mechanism. No writer worth reading just 'takes it from real life' but transmutes experience through his special vision; that is the essential difference between journalism and writing novels. Even the least ambitious class of novel is more than a mere report of facts. The writer's own memory and subconscious are therefore his prime sources of concepts. I was once present when a Famous Writer moaned to a Respected Elder of our profession that he had 'written himself out'; minutes later, the Famous Writer had us laughing with a hilarious story about grenade instruction gone wrong while he was in the military. The Respected Elder stopped him cold: 'You're wasting the central set piece of a great comic novel on two listeners when you could be telling it to sixty thousand hardcover readers and collecting royalties.' The Famous Writer left his drink unfinished in his hurry to reach his typewriter. In fact, the grenade-training incident didn't feature in the novel when it was finished and it wasn't a comedy at all, but the incident from his memory gave him the impetus to weave an intricate tale and write his book. Though one would, of course, not ask another writer about such a thing, my feeling is that the grenade-training incident was too close to the bone for him personally to write about – but it brought to mind other characters, other incidents, which time and the mysterious processes of the mind had modified and which his great skill further transmuted and, eventually, there was his novel.

Besides the themes (here in the sense of a concept or idea, rather than a fully developed and detailed plot outline) you carry in your memory, there are possibilities all around you. Look to your neighbours. Is one married to an older woman? Why? Who has a car way beyond his means? How does he afford it? Do colleagues at work have secret dreams and lusts? Newspapers, television, radio are all bonanzas for the writer in search of a plot idea. And don't just stick to the headlines, try the small fillers inside, the human interest touches, the obituaries (a goldmine), the background articles and current affairs programmes. I'm not suggesting you become a newshound: I don't take a daily paper, do not watch television for ten months in the year (Len Deighton doesn't have a television at all because its absence gives him an extra day a week in which to write), read the news magazines and yachting monthlies every quarter at the dentist, and the motoring and computer magazines at the library once a month. But I am perfectly well informed from a thorough reading of a Sunday paper say six times a year and from listening to BBC Radio 4 whenever I'm in the car or lunching in my study. There is no *need* for you to become a newshound – if something is important to you, eventually you will find out about it. Andrew McCoy dines out on the tale of how his editor, John Blackwell, in a Soho pub near closing time one night, turned to him and said, 'D'ya shee the shtory of the elepshants onna box lassni'? We'll commishionna novelbout bloody ivory, lash elepshants.' It turned out Blackwell hadn't seen the programme himself and that it had been screened six weeks before but someone had told the editor about it in the pub the night before. Editor and author finally found another tippler who had seen the programme, a current affairs production about elephants being in danger of total extinction, and received a vague second-hand description of the facts. From this unpromising seed, believe it or not, grew *Blood Ivory*. Another example: someone suggested to me I do a book about terrorists holding hostages at the top of a skyscraper and gave me chapter and verse, obtained from an engineer at his club, on how a properly qualified sapper could blow down a skyscraper floor by floor, without in the least disturbing the occupants (it was of course a windowless skyscraper) until the top floor sat at ground level and could be stormed by the police. I didn't take greatly to this idea because it required too much suspension of disbelief from readers but asked if I could have the technical details for my own. Six weeks later that monster sinkhole in Florida hit the news and in a flash I saw how blowing down a skyscraper gently could be a chief ornament of a disaster novel about a *Sinkhole*.

The non-fiction section of your library is another goldmine. The writer's mainstays are biography, history, politics, economics, psychology, travel; but I've also had ideas from the aeronautics shelves and a book on woodworking.

New writers often ask, 'What if someone else has the same idea at the same time?' The answer is 'So what?' (There are various registers to avoid duplicating *non-fiction* books.) It really doesn't matter because your novels will all be different and, unless tied to a very specific event, as described under the next heading, there will not be an instant glut on the market obvious to all publishers. For instance, there are five or six novels, all conceived and written at approximately the same time and published within a few years of each other, all built around the answer to the question 'How does a man like Kim Philby retire without one side or the other killing him?' A more diverse bunch of answers to the same question would be hard to imagine.

This brings us to the last source of ideas for writers: other people's fiction. Suppose you read my own solution to the Philby riddle, *Reverse Negative*, and decide you can write a better thriller around the Philby/Fourth Man conundrum. There is absolutely no reason why you shouldn't try your hand, as long as you do not lift plot *details* or *characterization* directly from another writer because that would be plagiarism and theft and actionable at law. However, by now, publishers will know of the several other Philby novels and, unless yours really has something new to say, you would be shooting yourself in the foot by even starting it. For this reason, it is normal to restrict concept-pilfering from other authors to the throwaway side issues in which any good novel abounds but which suggest to you a complete central theme.

Too-popular plots

There are some plot ideas you should not touch. One publisher, at whose office incoming manuscripts are placed on the hat rack to be collected by publishers' readers, calls them hat-rack breakers.

The Iranian and Beirut hostage crises are examples of themes hundreds of aspirant writers took up because of the pervasive publicity, huge public interest and general availability of the facts; six months to a year after these events, the hat racks were groaning under such novels and, even if they were all different (and the closer they stuck to reality, the less different they could be), only a handful could be published before public surfeit triumphed. If you choose such a subject, you're loading the dice against yourself. But, if such an event suggests to you a novel about the larger underlying questions of Beirut and the Middle East, then your effort will be judged on its own merits. I bet the Middle East novels of those wily old professionals Le Carré and Leon Uris will be selling long after the instant-hostage books have been recycled.

Check whose books succeeded after Desert Storm, the war with Iraq to liberate Kuwait. The books that sold were either by those who had relevant experience in that war such as special forces soldiers, or by established professionals such as Frederic Forsyth and Gavin Lyall, who wrote my favourite, *Uncle Target*, with a very clever, claustrophobic angle, using an established character of great depth, Major Harry Maxim. Personally, I sat in front of my television night after night, cursing CNN and the BBC for bringing solutions to plots directly into people's homes as fast as I thought them up. I proposed no thriller about that war to any publisher, and declined to write the one that was offered to me because I thought the plot idea would throw up cardboard characters; I heard later that others also turned it down, and that the writer who eventually accepted it did his career no good whatsoever when the book failed.

It is easy to understand the Iranian, Beirut and Iraqi examples because we have the perspective of history; we can all see that those aspirants, and even some professionals, should have thought more carefully. But the same applies to the most earth-shaking events in today's newspapers, television and radio news. As I write this (first full week of January 1999), President Clinton is being tried under articles of impeachment by the Senate. That is clearly a huge story, but it is too late for most of us to hitch a ride on the bandwagon because smarter authors saw it coming months or even years ago and sold all the books which could be sold on the subject. Next time it becomes a viable subject will be for reporters' and historians' accounts. To get a quote, I called an agent, not my own but one who has known me for several years, and said, 'I want to ask you a question about the Clinton trial.' She screamed! When she calmed down, and still under the impression I wanted to suggest a book to her, she said, 'You'd better have an angle so far out nobody has ever thought of it, André, otherwise you're wasting your dime and my time.' An hour later she called me back and said, 'Didn't you once write a screenplay about the moral issues behind the election of Eisenhower? You should speak to your man in LA, because right now the quality film makers are running around frantically looking for a pathfinder through the moral maze of this mess, a writer who can turn politics into screen action. Maybe that track record is worth a film deal. But a book? Forget it!' Our conversations together lasted perhaps five or six minutes, but she put her finger on all three problems: when something as big as the Clinton trial is already in the news it is too late to suggest the book, there is a glut before the event has even happened except for those with a really far-out angle (which will probably not attract a huge readership precisely because it is odd), and only those with a relevant track record can even get a hearing. She also identified the one opportunity in the affair, but one which applies to only a very limited

number of thriller writers: that the other media may offer opportunities already closed to books – which is irrelevant to readers
of this book because they're trying to break into books, not to
vault the much higher barriers to screenwriting. And you may
be certain the major deals in films, as in books, are already cut
and dried; it will be the smaller film makers who are still looking for a writer. She told me something else of interest: that she
was looking for a romance writer to write a love story featuring
a female reporter and *set against* the trial, an idea she already
had a publisher for. That opportunity, to use the background of
the trial to add tension to other stories, will also stand for
thriller writers for years to come.

Finally, there are plots in the news that have become worn
through over-use. I would not today start a book about a serial
killer unless I was convinced that my angle was utterly compelling. Surely I cannot be the only reader who is fed up with
killers who kill for the sake of killing, no matter how interestingly odd the detectives who hunt them. Yet that is what serial
killer thrillers have now almost universally descended to.
Climbing Everest because it is there was interesting when
Edmund Hillary said it, but in serial killers it is a motive worn
beyond credibility by repetition.

The permissible limits

Novelists are permitted 'borrowing' that would elsewhere be
called theft. Indeed, such cross-pollination of ideas is not only
permitted but should be encouraged for the health of the literary
form. Fiction writers work almost uniquely with other people's
hypotheses, research, facts and conclusions. The art and originality of the storyteller lie to a far greater extent in how he puts his
tale together than in its content and can, arguably, be defined as
giving a new twist to an old story. There are said to be only
seven completely original plots but they can all be resurrected
many times by peopling them with different characters.

If you should not take detailed plots and characters from
other fiction writers, what may you take and from whom?

You may take detailed plots and characters from non-fiction
writers, as long as the plots and characters are from life – that
is, from biography or history. However, you cannot merely

fictionalize another writer's work episode by episode: your novel should contain more and different scenes and characters which you can only add if there are several more books on the same subject or if you did independent research of your own or added very substantial imagery of your own. For safety, your work should never depend solely or even substantially on a single non-fiction source. You should ask permission from the publishers to quote any text (fiction, non-fiction, poetry, song lyrics) with the exception of those classics which are now out of copyright.

If in doubt, take legal advice. Most authors' associations will advise either gratis or for a nominal fee on simple questions and tell you when it is necessary to refer to more expert opinion; I've always had my copyright advice free of charge from the Australian Copyright Council (who are obviously not responsible for anything I say in this book).

Commonplace and notebooks

A commonplace book is one in which the keeper writes down striking phrases and lines read elsewhere; some writers use such books for inspiration. Many writers also keep notebooks of their own ideas, of felicitous phrases they think up or overhear, of concepts, etc. You could try these but I consider them a waste of time. What I do think essential is that, every time a concept strikes you, *you write it down immediately*. A single line on a sheet of paper will do. (I keep my single sheets in a three-inch thick file labelled 'Ideas'.) This will preserve the central kernel of the idea until the light of morning or until you get around to it. Otherwise these concepts will either fly from your mind before you want them again or weasel into something that lacks the spark which fires a whole novel. If you have a dictaphone, keep it by your bedside and transcribe the ideas of the dawn every day before you start work.

Pressures proper and improper

In the old days, in order to complete your apprenticeship successfully, it helped to be seen in the approved church at the regulated times. The modern author is subject to the same compulsion of conformity of belief and as many, if different, classes of behaviour are likely to be punished as they were for the Victorian apprentice.

In general, writers are assumed to be of liberal-humanist or left-wing outlook because that describes the literary industry (academics, critics, publishers, publicists, self-promoters, proselytizers and poseurs). This is a gross misrepresentation, for novelists do in fact share political views spanning the ideological compass. However, it would be amiss of me not to tell you that it is easier to be published if you seem to profess, through your leading characters' actions, a moderate, liberal viewpoint. If you don't believe me, try finding a publisher for a novel presenting Hitler's cohorts or John Birch right-wing racists in a favourable light. I can think of only one truly racist novel being published in my lifetime, and that happened in France.

The political position is nowhere near as bad as in the 1930s when the Communists openly threatened Fredric Warburg with the ruination of his publishing house if he didn't suppress 'the renegade' Orwell, but writers of the outspoken right do still receive a noticeably rougher critical ride than those of the radical left. Thus, if viewpoints outside the narrow pale of Western liberal-humanism are essential to your story, prudence dictates that the opposing view be at least presented (say by another character).

How far you heed such pressures is a function of your commitment to what you have to say. You need not bend at all, you can say exactly what you want and, if you write interestingly, your book will eventually be published. Most authors probably don't mind bending a little before pressures they consider insignificant or merely commercial good sense, but would most definitely draw a line and take a stand on principle somewhere else.

Women are the most frequent readers and buyers of books – yes, even of thrillers. Women are increasingly taking over important editorial positions. The author who wants to be published will take account of these marketing considerations.

It is, however, one thing voluntarily to avoid irrelevant male chauvinism because it is ill manners, but another to bow before pressures antipathetic to artistic liberty. Witness the ludicrous attempt by a group of militant feminists in editorial positions in a New York publishing house to suppress one of Kingsley Amis's novels: this is straightforward literary thuggery akin to the brutish censorship of the Italian printers who, after the Second World War, by striking and sabotaging presses every time they were faced with a book critical of Communism, forced Italian publishers to decline all such books (a practice so widespread that it acquired its own name, 'the hegemonization of publishing'). Authors with commercial sense will avoid publishing managements so weak as to allow malicious malcontents in their own midst free rein to pervert normal editorial and marketing practice; such managements are not likely to stand by their author if some other bunch of fringe maniacs should decide to attack his novels.

There are characters and plots that virtually guarantee you won't be published. An Uncle Tom black character is likely to get you a rejection letter today just as a depiction of an unscrupulous and incompetent doctor would have done a hundred years ago (and even a couple of decades ago on the BBC).

Other items liable to pre-censorship and self-censorship vary from time to time and according to where you want to sell your wares. These no-noes are grandly referred to by publishers as 'the received wisdom of the profession' but they're really self-fulfilling prophecies and prejudices. They include (at the end of the century) 'ice stories' for film in Los Angeles, African stories in New York, right-wing attitudes or Marxist texts for popular consumption in either New York or London, at several publishers thrillers set in a time (roughly 50–75 years ago) too near to be 'historical' and not far enough into the past to be nostalgic, and so on down to particular editorial prejudices ('I can't abide spooks,' one editor told me when I suggested a quality ghost story) which can be as important if you have spent several years building up your relationship with one publisher in the hope that eventually he will publish you.

There is very little that I can usefully say about the amount of violence, sex or foul language that is permissible, because this is both technically and aesthetically an irrelevant question; and in any event the acceptability of violence, sex and foul language runs in cycles. My own formula is to use violence, sex and foul language whenever it is justified and, if an editor objects, he must prove a literary rather than ethical or commercial case to convince me part or all should be removed. But you should read passim in this book where I speak of emotional commitment, and study carefully the section in John Braine's book where he deals with sex, because it is very easy for sex scenes to degenerate into pornography. On the other hand, if they are essential to your story, don't shirk them or readers will know you for a moral coward.

The difficulty the author faces with politically unpopular depictions, as with violence, sex and foul language, is that 'telling it like it is' constitutes no defence, because partisan critics and literary thugs alike inhabit that normative dreamland where what should be is myopically substituted for what is.

You must decide for yourself whether you want to be right and unpopular or whether you will flow with the tide; the difference between proper and improper editorial pressure on your choice and treatment of material is that proper pressure tends to the situation where no (or very few) publishers will publish the resulting novel, while improper pressure will emanate from only a few publishers, and those usually fringe ones, leaving you a wide choice. There may also still be a very few publishers who are so convinced of the need for literary freedom that they will publish novels against the mainstream of contemporary opinion, even if they do not themselves agree with the opinions expressed, simply because they are good novels.

However, in today's conglomerate publishing world, even if you are more likely to be irritated by demands for political correctness on trivialities, you are probably more likely to have a book espousing an outrageously unconventional opinion taken on by a publisher who hopes that the controversy will be newsworthy and thus generate sales, than you were when publishers pretended to a morality beyond profits. Not all progress is bad!

Literary imperialism

A problem that used to affect writers outside London and New York was that of literary centralism – and this sometimes extended to a virtual restriction on the setting of a novel, to plot and character choice. Fortunately this is no longer the case, and indeed it is possible that it may be a positive advantage for the aspiring writer to live in the country, in another city, even in one of the colonies or points more exotic because editors seem to be on the lookout for new viewpoints and new settings. The world has become a village and, as long as your plots are not of only narrow regional interest, you will command greater conviction if you set them in places you know (but see Chapter 7 on Research).

4. Breathing Life into Characters

Characters are the glue that sticks the parts of your novel together and the umbilical cord that holds your reader's attention. Characters explicate concepts in action, characters by their actions expound your plot, characters (rather than plots) provide the emotional link – 'identification' in the jargon – between your reader and your theme and are consequently the main motivators of tension. Therefore, effective creation and presentation of characters are the most important of your writing skills. Without effective characters, there will be no reader identification, without reader identification no tension – and without tension, no novel, never mind a thriller. More, the modern thriller writer requires greater skill in character creation than the 'straight' novelist; this is because the increased respectability of the better thrillers has been won at the cost of having the highest critical standards applied to nearly all thrillers, and the difficulty is compounded by the requirement for pace which inevitably imposes very tight space restrictions on characterization.

How high should you aim?

All that said, various classes of thrillers require different levels of skill with characterization. The classic locked room mystery can still get away, though only barely, with cardboard characters because the main thing is the puzzle, but even here it is noticeable that the characters of even the worst offenders are decidedly less stiff than, say, those in the whodunnits of pre-War authors. Equally, because pace is paramount in the adventure story which is generally accepted as being modestly less sophisticated than the thriller, readers and most professional critics will, if the tale is otherwise exceptional, make allowances for skimpily sketched characters. However, charity does not invariably prevail, and you could find your work unfavourably compared with that of a top professional adventure writer, say Wilbur Smith, who has both excellent quickly sketched characters and riveting pace. It would therefore be self-defeating to select your place in the spectrum of thrillers according to your present skill at characterization. Far better to write what you want to write and to work at improving your characterization, not only to the required minimum but to the highest achievable level; if your characterization is richer than expected in your chosen class of thriller, so much the better for your chances of publication.

Character v. pace

If, in the early stages of your apprenticeship, you are faced with a choice between characterization and pace, choose to round the character at the expense of pace; you can always come back later and cut or compress to enhance the pace – a much simpler matter, as I will show in Chapter 9, than trying to blow the spark of life into a character who was stillborn or grew up deprived. Do not despair: the skill of quick, even instant, characterization is, like all the others, learnt rather than inherent. Perseverance will triumph.

You know all your characters already

Only God can create a character from scratch so that the new person bears absolutely no relation to anyone He ever met or read about. Some writers may sincerely believe this is what they do. But many know that the process of creating characters from a handful of dust does not stand close examination while true faith in this miracle (as contrasted to lip service induced by fear of the libel laws) can be an important impediment to the regular and consistent creation of varied, individual characters. The professional writer, who must create a new set of characters at least once a year, cannot depend on the lottery of inspiration. In any event, 'inspiration' is merely the convenient name for doing subconsciously what we here propose to do more efficiently with our wits about us.

Concept characters

A number of characters will be inherent in the concept. These may or may not be your central character(s). It was obvious from the start that my disaster novel *Sinkhole*, about a city falling into a hole in the ground, would, or at least could have, characters from the police, fire, hospital and other emergency services; if the disaster were bad enough, the National Guard would be called out; journalists would cover the disaster. However, while people from all these organizations had substantial parts, I chose to make my hero a car salesman and part-time mountaineer because my concept was to tell the story from the spearhead of the rescue attempts rather than from the command or even national (Washington) viewpoint. Now, I can state categorically that I have never met a mountaineering car salesman. That is the truth, and nothing but the truth – but is it whole? No, it is not: I have met and read about many mountaineers; in advertising I worked with and collected tales about a great many car salesmen, from corner used-car lots right up to Henry Ford. Even the name I chose for my hero was suggested to me by no fewer than three men I know who were christened Quinten and hate the name. None of these facts are listed in my notes for the novel and it took me a while to dredge them out of my memory; you may be certain there are other indicators locked into my subconscious that I have not managed to unearth.

Character transmutation

The character each of us knows best is our own and, by extension, it is often said that the characters in an author's novel are merely representations of the varied facets of himself. There is a kernel of truth in this – and the introspective navel-novels that so blight our literary epoch are extreme cases – but most authors instinctively command the common sense to transform what they know at first hand through the filter of observed real world experience: people in their own families, at work, in the street, on the bus or train, in the news, in biographies and histories, in other people's fiction. The process can be either subconscious or conscious and consists of taking something from here and something from there until you have a coherent whole. Further differentiation between characters is provided in the writing by their attitudes, actions, dialogue and so on, the mechanics of which we shall come to.

Libel

You must not in your novels name real people as characters, or describe them in such a way that they may be recognized. If you do, and the actions ascribed to them are such that they may be held up to ridicule or suffer loss in their community or profession, you may be liable for damages or even be imprisoned. Even if no evil is ascribed to their characters in your novel, their mere appearance in it (can you *guarantee* some bilious critic won't call your novel a 'disreputable travesty'?) may bring them into disrepute and therefore be actionable. Don't!

Don't, even in jest, threaten to put your friends in your novels. They may no longer be your friends when, ten years hence, your subconscious drags up some characteristic of the friend, sticks it on the baddie in your current novel and forgets to inform your conscious mind until the writ arrives.

Don't use names from the telephone book for your characters. Use town names from a gazetteer (at the back of a geographical or road atlas) instead, then check in the voters' roll for the town your story is set in that no-one of the name lives there (the telephone book is second-best if you can't get hold of the voters' roll); if you give a character a profession, you should also check that no-one of that name practises the profession anywhere in the *country* where the story is set; finally, you should check *all* names (persons, companies, organizations, institutions) against all the references and directories (*Who's Who*, Kelly's, etc.) your library has.

Don't quote the car licence number or telephone number of any character without first ascertaining from the appropriate authorities that such numbers are non-existent; many authorities have a reserve of numbers used only in fiction from which they will allocate you one if you ask politely. Heed the lesson of the famous story about the television writer/director who, up against a deadline, used his own licence plate on the car driven by the actor playing the child molester in a piece of television only a moron could mistake for anything but fiction. The week after the episode was screened, the writer and his car (with his registration plate back on it) were attacked in the High Street of his village by shoppers who did substantial damage before the police arrived and explained he wasn't wanted for child-molesting. The likely libel damages if he had used someone else's number do not bear thinking about.

In most places in the world, ignorance or the absence of malicious intent is *not* a defence against libel, but proof that you checked to the very best of your ability that you were libelling no-one may be taken as a mitigating circumstance. In some countries a defence against a charge of libel is possible by proving disclosures were made in the public interest, which of course implies an admission of intent to libel, and the onus of proof then falls on the libeller (the accused – you), a prospect that turns the staunchest legal stomach.

When you get your first publishing contract, you will find its most horrifying clause, and the only one which no publisher will allow you to delete or alter, gives the publisher an unconditional guarantee that you will foot the bill for damages and legal costs in any case involving obscenity, defamation or libel. If publishers are scared sick, it behoves mere authors to tread carefully.

Now let us denigrate great men and famous

In theory at least, you can say what you like about dead men; in practice there are ways in which the surviving relatives of people defamed, especially if they are rich and well connected, can act against you.

It is also contemporary practice to include the living great in modern novels, not just as representative of the great office they hold, but often by their given names and described by their peculiarities either lovable or disgraceful, according to the author's inclination. As a rule, it is beneath the dignity of such men (and Lady Thatcher) to sue mere novelists but there is no legal bar to their doing so. Twenty years ago a lawyer I met socially gleefully volunteered the frightening information that Yuri Andropov, then Chairman of the KGB, should he desire to retire a multi-millionaire in the West, need only sue me and a dozen other thriller writers *and our rich publishers* (if lawyers know writers have no money, then the KGB knows too) for libelling him in our novels.

Plot flows from character

The greatest care is required in choosing and delineating your characters, because so much follows. In particular, the twists and turns of the detailed plot will owe a great deal to the friction between the characters and to their opposing goals. Take *Sinkhole*: it is wisdom after the event, with the book written, to say that the chief character could have succeeded only through unflagging drive and an obstinate unwillingness to be beaten back by petty bureaucrats and nature alike. But, when I created the character, I did not make him a mountaineer because I knew he would need an indomitable will in bureaucratic battles – it was the other way round: I first gave him an indomitable will and then made him a mountaineer (as second choice to a potholer or spelunker because Trevanian's *Shibumi* had just appeared) because I already knew something about the techniques of mountaineering and could present it convincingly. From there, the next step was that such a man (especially if he was self-made, hence his profession as a car distributor) would not let petty bureaucrats deter him long and, since the concept itself suggested there would be some bureaucrats, one major strand of human conflict developed from the single word I wrote down as my player's leading characteristic: 'iron-willed'. This is, of course, an ultra-simplified version of what happened: in reality I had many choices – my strong-willed hero could be in conflict with bureaucracy (two kinds in the novel as published), another strong-willed rescuer with different priorities, his own conscience (by rescuing some from certain death, he risks others), one or more of the victims, members of his own team challenging for the leadership. What all these possible strands of conflict have in common is that they involve other people and their characteristics.

Naming your characters

Many professional novelists agonise over the choice of names for their characters and with good cause. Suppose Ian Fleming had called 007 Isadore Wimp, do you suppose his books would have sold? George Smiley sounds like a regular guy, Bill Hayden rolls off the tongue as being slightly suspicious and not quite British before one finds out anything else about him, Toby

Esterhase is obviously an untrustworthy creepy-crawly, and Karla implies something sly and vicious and treacherous – exactly what I would call an Alsatian dog! Joe Lampton could only be a coal miner or a Yorkshireman on the make; if he were a pattern-maker or precision-moulder, he would be called Albert, full out, not Al or Bert, and you'd have to drop the Lampton because Albert Lampton doesn't ring euphoniously whereas Joe Lampton has an admirable inevitability. An important editor says a felicitous selection of character names is one of the handful of criteria he considers in those ten or fewer pages he reads of unsolicited novels that wash in over the transom (his brutal metaphor, not mine); if the names are wrong, he won't read on, if they're right and nothing else is obviously incompetent, he might read on.

Writing down characters

Just as you wrote down your concept, so you should write down your characters. John Braine suggests a minimum: age, physical appearance, profession, ages of children, etc. – and to keep notes as brief as possible. I read Braine's book *Writing a Novel* only after I finished the first draft of this book but I wish I had had that advice when I started out as a novelist. Then I wrote reams of character descriptions extraneous to the thriller itself. An utter waste. What you want is one side of a sheet of paper per character to keep beside you to refer to during the detailed plotting and perhaps while you write the novel. Don't try to fill the sheet; just write down what you consider essential.

From this point, I shall assume you have read this book once through to find your bearings and you are now in the process of writing your novel and referring back to this chapter for help when you run into a problem of characterization.

Stop that character, it is running away!

The reason long character descriptions are such a waste is that character, for the narrative novelist in general but in particular for the thriller writer who has less space for character development, is created most satisfactorily not in description but in *action*. Even at its most basic, defining a man by his possessions, it is dull to write, 'He had a Bentley Turbo,' and hardly more inspired to show him driving routinely to his office in it, but riveting to show him racing across Germany in it to save the girl while being chased by baddies in equally fast cars. There are two considerations here: _relevance to character_ and _relevance to action_. In the first two examples, the car may be relevant to the character to show either wealth or snobbery – and then should be better handled in the second sense of relevance. In the chase example the car is relevant to the action and tells us as much about the character as in the other examples – but in addition the car furthers the plot and creates a thrill for the reader.

It is a trap to conclude from this that only those characteristics that may be described in action should find a place in your novel but you should, in the interest of pace, search very hard for ways to build a fully rounded character as largely as possible in action and in friction with other characters rather than lying on his bed examining his own navel. The only time to back off (should you be so fortunate as to arrive at this point) is where the character and the reader are seeing too much action without pause for breath or thought. What you do then depends on the cause: too much plot, the most common cause, you fix by cutting and saving the surplus events for your next novel. In that rare case where your character is so complex that he won't fit the confines of whatever length you are writing to (60–100,000 words are your best bet), you must then simply go to greater length or contrive to squeeze more character development into each activity. Other remedies are canvassed in Chapter 9.

'Right' and 'wrong' characters

'Wrong' characters are wallflowers at the party: they relate to no-one else, they don't spark off anybody, nobody wants to know their secrets (now that _defines_ dull), and they suggest nothing interesting they can do either with or in opposition to the leading characters. If they are your leading characters, you're in trouble and must start again because you've gone wrong somewhere. This is fortunately a rare occurrence; far more commonly they are subsidiary characters and by their very uselessness declare their irrelevance to the story you're telling. Write them out.

'Right' characters are different: they sparkle with contradictions, they spark off all the other characters but especially the main characters, whom they also complement like spoons in a drawer; they have secrets and hidden dreams that others would pay to discover; in a word, they are interesting, not dull, perhaps even fascinating. An elevated, even exalting, state of 'rightness' arises when a character self-generates so much plot that you can barely keep him under control, a process known derogatively as 'the character running away with the author'. (You'd be a very poor specimen if you couldn't control a character you had yourself created on paper rather than in a laboratory.) Such characters are a joy and a pleasure and almost write the books they appear in. You collect such characters by living body and soul with your writing, thinking about your characters every moment that you can find, worrying at them like a dog at a bone for that last little scrap of interaction with the other characters and the reasons behind it.

But beware, many 'overwritten' novels (a fatal description in editorial offices) result from the author's fascination with and pleasure in just such appealing characters; by all means write it all down but be prepared to murder your darlings ruthlessly if they hold up the forward momentum of the action.

Now for the bad news: you can't find out about the right and wrong characters without actually writing the story. It is impossible to find those characters you can or should do without except by creating them on paper at some considerable length. And, since they won't reveal themselves except in relevant action, you cannot do this in some dry description apart from the story you want to tell, you must do it in your novel. This is one advantage of the 'John Braine method' (see next chapter) of writing a complete first draft at high speed before coming back to refine character descriptions and plot outline prior to writing a completely new draft; all the dud characters can be eliminated in a draft you are already resigned to scrapping.

Dull characters

There is another class of characters. They would, in real life, be worthy people, they may even in your novel be worthwhile characters, but they suffer from a terminal illness: they bore *you* stiff. An author who has no feeling either sympathetic or antipathetic to a character does not present a neutral depiction – there is no such thing – but a boring one. If you find a character bores you, don't try to jazz it up because your readers won't be fooled; get rid of it.

Contrasts and foils

You should, however, differentiate intrinsically boring characters from those which serve, usually in minor parts, as contrasts or foils to your leading characters; for instance, in *Sinkhole* I deliberately created a neurotic housewife (whose stupid hopelessness depressed me terribly) as a mirror to the cheerful self-reliance of her friend who is one of the victims waiting to be rescued. The negative effect of such necessary characters can be minimized by showing them always in action and as briefly as will convey the point. Don't misunderstand me; there is no need to become the Norman Vincent Peale of the thriller world – if you want to present negative characters who are relevant to the story and for whom you feel sympathy (or antipathy), fine, but not characters who bore you-the-writer.

The good guys and the bad guys

It is coarsely held to be axiomatic that the writer is in perfect empathy with the hero and to lesser degrees with the other good guys; the writer is also taken to be 'agin' the bad guys. Axiomatic, that is, in the crudest kind of Western. The modern thriller offers this dichotomy only at its very lowest levels. Loyalty and guilt, courage and patriotism, faith and cynicism, friendship and love, are more subtly layered the higher one ascends the ladder until, at the top, it is often very difficult indeed to decipher whose side the author is on, if he is indeed on anyone's – and sometimes even if there are sides! I don't for a moment suppose authors choose their own position on this scale. Instead, it seems to me that their skill at creating and presenting ever more complex characters at the same time increases the subtlety of their narrative. If you read in chronological order the books of a serious author (McCarry, rather than Ludlum) you like and admire, the development becomes clear. With others, you will find a high point and then a decline which often coincides with bestsellerdom and uncritical acceptance. ('Oh, that's because he believes his own publicity,' a Grand Old Man told me when I complained that the latest from his friend the Famous Author was poor stuff.)

This subtlety is of course worthless if practised for its own sake and when clumsily done is mere obscurantism soon recognized and damned by readers for its pompous pretence. But, if it flows from a genuine understanding of all characters, good, bad or indifferent (but not boring!), that is, as a result rather than a mere mechanical cause, it is a Good Thing. Unfortunately, study of the leading texts reveals amazingly little to the novice, except how easily Len Deighton or Victor Canning gets away with breaking most of the rules in this book and every other book on the subject – the prerogative of the master craftsman.* Subtlety is not a technique in itself but an effect. How then to know and present your characters so that their actions and the frictions between them accurately reflect your own growing perception of the issues underlying the visible plot – and in the process exalt your writing step by step until one day it bears comparison with the masters?

We have already seen three tools the professionals apply, whether this is done consciously or has become second nature through long practice. These are: avoidance of the blunt, dull statement; the use of contrast, preferably graded – the narrower the scale of these gradations yet the greater their number, the greater the subtlety; and the exclusion of dull characters for whom the author has no feeling, either for or against.

Viewpoints

The point from which the writer, and perforce his reader, views the tale to be told reflects his attitude to each of his characters. There is no such thing as an author who is truly neutral to his characters but there are ways of pretending more or less successfully that you are giving every character the same amount of time at the bat. Equally, there are ways in which your commitment to a certain character or small group of characters may be signalled to your reader.

The author's viewpoint owes its primacy in classroom and other structured literary discussion to its obvious utility as an analytical device. But the practising author, and especially the novice, does not normally use it as a constructional tool, simply

---

*This, and other advanced matters, is discussed in Chapter 6.

because the point of view usually comes to him as part of the concept. As with the tone of voice, discussed elsewhere, a decision about point of view is usually thrust upon the writer only when things go awry in the writing. If you realize late in the novel that you are telling the story from the wrong character's point of view, this often also means you're telling the wrong story (because a different 'hero' will lead the story in different directions) and you will probably have to start afresh. The other, and fortunately most common, point at which you will have to face the choice arises when you wish to include something invisible from the existing viewpoint; at this stage you will suddenly become aware that it is possible to change viewpoints even in mid-narrative and can select one or more of those listed below. As for the advice sometimes offered that the novelist should decide his point of view as a planning procedure, I doubt the efficacy of this counsel for any but the most professional novelists and then only for their simplest and most straightforward books. By all means consider the possibilities but don't torture yourself with them; in your original draft, follow your first inclination and tell it the way it seems natural – you'll find out soon enough if you go wrong.

First person

The first-person narrative provides instant identification with the hero for both author and reader. Even when the 'I' of the tale is less than savoury, the implication is that his circumstances allow of no better behaviour, or that only the hard-hearted would condemn a man so charming for a few small peccadilloes (think of an Eric Ambler hero). This approach at first seems to hold many attractions for the new novelist. After all, the narrative form we most practise is 'And then I did so and so'; many plotting problems melt away for the first person narrator; the requirements of several differentiated and rounded characters and of character contrasts become less acute; and the changes in outlook inherent in many other narrative techniques, which are in themselves stumbling blocks for the novice struggling to control a single viewpoint, are eliminated.

Unfortunately, the first-person narrative has very great disadvantages too: plotting can become very difficult when there seems no way to introduce certain information to the narrator without ludicrous contortions either by him or another character; the requirement that a first-person narrator feels so much more deeply and experiences the events of the story so much more acutely than characters with whom the reader identifies less closely can trip up even experienced authors; characterization, unless controlled with a very firm hand, can more easily than in other formats encroach on space better reserved for action. It is true that in one of my earliest novels, *Reverse Negative*, I knew no better than to use a first-person narrator but, to keep the story under control, I was soon driven to include computer-generated probability studies* of what the other characters were doing. There is no doubt that most of my problems with that novel stemmed from the use of first-person narrative; conversely when, a dozen novels later, I tackled a sequel, my greater experience helped me keep the computer syntheses down to less than one tenth of the narrative as compared with nearly half in the earlier book.

After a quarter-century of additional experience, I write this revision of *Writing a Thriller* right after finishing a first-person novel in which the first-person viewpoint is in fact one of the narrative deceptions which builds the tension for the audience. That is something I might have contemplated back then, and which would certainly have destroyed my book with complications that I could with limited experience then neither have foreseen nor handled. The experience confirms my belief that the beginner who chooses the first-person viewpoint should do so only for fairly simple, straighforward stories.

Single third-person
A compromise that offers most of the benefits and avoids almost all the pitfalls of first-person narrative is the single-person view-

---

*If you know how a certain individual behaved under known historical circumstances, you can feed this information to a computer together with information on how people in general or others in his profession react to various stimuli. You can then have the computer tell you how the chosen individual will behave in different but related hypothetical circumstances or probably did behave in known but unobserved circumstances. The computer's answers are normally, in the versions used by commercial and national security organizations, in the form of a number of possible responses graded by their statistical probability. Tables and graphs qualified by confidence levels are of course not the stuff of tension (quite apart from readers' inability to interpret them) so I cheated by presenting these probability studies as narratives 'written' by the computer.

point, where everything is seen through the eyes of the leading character, who is, however, distanced from the narrator by being 'he' rather than 'I'. A good example is Andrew Garve's *A Hero for Leanda* (in large print if your library's copy of the original edition has been read to pieces), where we are given absolutely nothing the hero doesn't experience first-hand or isn't told within the reader's hearing.

God's-eye view
The most common narrative form is the god's-eye view (third person impersonal in the jargon) where the author shows each character when his actions are relevant to the story and fills gaps in the essential fabric of knowledge for the reader. In prac-tice, this viewpoint follows, and identifies with, one or a very small number of characters who enjoy the author's implicit approval. It is such a common form because it offers the best of all worlds to both author and reader but, please, don't choose it automatically without considering whether one of the admit-tedly more difficult viewpoints would not be more apt to the story you are about to tell.

Equal time
A far more difficult – and very unusual – version of the god's-eye view is that in which the author bends over backwards to be fair to all his characters; here each receives not only equal time but an equal entitlement to the balance of doubt for his argument. This approach is most suited to the higher reaches of the thriller, where moral questions are canvassed. It is ferociously difficult to be fair to all characters because the author, however hard he tries, is never truly neutral. However, I suggest that you try and write at least one draft of your novel from this viewpoint, because it will exercise your growing skill in another direction, that of giving the baddies a credible voice of their own.

Cheating readers
Red herrings are admirable, cheating readers deplorable. A red herring is set up by a thoroughly motivated action that is *in character* with the character performing it and which directs the reader's eye away from the real culprit. Cheating occurs when the author breaks faith with the reader. If you do not take your

reader inside a character's thoughts, fine, the readers know what to expect. But, once you've invited your reader into a character's head, you have made a commitment to tell the reader everything relevant to the story going on in that character's mind, unless you've somehow made it clear that the visit won't be repeated. For instance, Noel Hynd's otherwise excellent *False Flags* is spoilt because he repeatedly takes us inside the head of one character and shows us everything she thinks except the most important part of her thoughts; and he shows us everything she does except the most important of her actions. Then, right at the end of his book we find out she's the guilty party. This is as much a cheat as deus ex machina; both author and editor are culpable for not cutting the offending sections which add nothing to the book.

Credible black hats

Of the many reasons why so many fictional baddies are cardboard cutouts, two are more culpable than the others: authors naturally identify with the good guys rather than the bad and, in most of the thriller classes accessible to the novice, the amount of space available for developing characters other than the leading one is extremely limited. At the lowest level of thrillers, cardboard baddies may well be accepted, even expected, by readers; this is the solace of the familiar and the professional author who scoffs at it is a snob. However, the market moves up all the time and this segment of it is in serious decline; aside from the commercial consideration, most aspirants will *want* to do better if they can.

The devil within?
It is important to understand that there is no such thing as a will to evil. Children up to five may tell you they will 'do bad things', but adults commit outrages against society or their fellow men from madness (psychopaths) or greed or need (common crime) or fear (violence) or ideological or chauvinist conviction (political crimes). Most might make a case, however cynical and shaky, that the means justify the end; even the vandal is inspired not by an urge to evil but by boredom or envy. I'm not constructing a Marxist argument that crime is society's fault, which is a matter

of definition, but that the perceptive author will see, not a crowd of hooligans destroying property for the sake of destruction, but a number of individuals with multiple individual motivations.

Two particularly irritating manifestations of 'will to evil' are found in novels about serial killers and the people who hunt them. The first is simply that authors made lazy by a few best-sellers throw up the stereotype 'serial killer' and then expect the reader to fill in the blanks. Serial killers, we are expected to believe, run around killing people because what they do is kill people. That's about as true was saying that Jews are usurers because they are Jews, or that journalists lie because they are journalists. An extreme form of this is the slackness of not even thinking up a new serial killer but simply reviving the original one from his gory end in the first book. The second manifest-ation is even more irritating. The serial killer is revived in a second book, but now he is not just hunting people to kill, he is hunting the hunter from the first book. Several novelists have recycled, not just once but several times, psychopaths whose new motive is to annihilate the hero-detective. Don't follow their bad example; you need to be a bestseller already to get away with shoddy work like that.

Humpbacks and nosedrips
Don't particularize your baddies by physical disabilities or peculiarities or by race alone. Sapper could count on kneejerk reflexes to huns, krauts, jerries and Jewish financiers with nasal drips; exactly the same characterizations will ensure that you remain unpublished.

Ways and means
In *Reverse Negative*, where my emotional commitment to the narrator was great – what else could it be when I was telling his story through his diary? – I finally overcame the disadvantage the black hats suffered because of this by writing the computer syntheses in which they appeared as a separate book seen from their viewpoint with the lot of them, traitors and innocent dupes, behaving absolutely righteously and in good faith as if they were the good guys and my diarist wore the black hat. Part of the strength of the book lies in this meeting of immovable object with irresistible force, so that the reader is torn between

conflicting loyalties almost to the end of the tale. However, this presupposes a narrative structure which can conveniently be split into two (or more) self-contained parts in its creation, to be merged later, and is therefore of limited application.

Another solution is to make your baddie rather likable, except for the single very serious character flaw which causes him to threaten to destroy the world or whatever. This is most easily done by demonstrating that he has the right instincts – through having the hero sympathize with some of his reasons for committing an outrage, for instance – but his means are despicable or out of proportion to the injustice he seeks to right. Karla, the Soviet spymaster in the Le Carré stories, becomes a sympathetic character even while he opposes the character we identify with, George Smiley, because the author chooses to tell us that Karla suffered for his commitment to his ideology by being imprisoned under Stalin and yet did not waver in his faith. Of course, Le Carré has created an admirable opponent rather than a likable one, but that merely requires greater skill; the principle is the same.

Character development

Fifty years ago, Ian Fleming's character James Bond was accepted without comment as a cad and a thug: already everyone knew which class of person became successful secret policemen and that the pre-War *beau idéal* was no longer tenable even in escapist fiction. But critics found Fleming's plots more than a little ludicrous. At the time, it was not thought worth much comment that Bond did not develop as a character through the book or even much over a series of books but it is doubtful if Bond would be such a huge success today. (The latterday continuation of the Bond saga by the excellent John Gardner conforms to modern practice by having Bond's character develop or, where that is impossible, by sending him up, and cannot be fairly compared to the originals, not least because Fleming altogether lacked Gardner's infectious sense of humour.) Plots that Fleming himself might have thought over the top are now breakfast commonplaces, taken from the media with our wheaties. There has also been a tenfold rise in the availability of the ersatz medium, television, which offers instant characterization (you like the actor's face or you don't) much more intimately in your living room than the big screen ever could and then fills the rest of the time with instant action. Partly in self-defence against exterior attack, and partly as an inevitable historical process of growth, the thriller has pulled itself up by its bootstraps in the eyes of both critics and readers. Improved character delineation was both a cause and an effect in this process. But that is not the way it is expressed: no-one in literature says, 'You must offer better delineated characters'; instead, we hear much about 'character development'.

As an aside, that is the loss of the novel. In film, stage and especially radio work, where the dialogue is everything, 'clearly delineated characters' is an essential concept. Not only is the idea *explicit* in discussions between the writer and those staging his work, but it carries the additional meaning of separation between characters, which is a tool which could usefully be imported to novels. See below about dialogue for the related concept of 'differentiation'.

Now, most of us have our own characters set in concrete before we are thirty and many of us are likely to laugh at those lost souls who, at forty, are still 'searching for the real me'. We *know* character does not develop much after one's teens, barring only major crises, and that even catastrophes are more likely to induce minor changes in personality (a mellowing, say) rather than a 180° conversion of the kind found in inspirational literature. Character development in the literary sense therefore implies something different from the common everyday meaning of the word (except when we are dealing with children and teenagers). What is this particular meaning, and how can the new author best portray developing characters? By measuring each character, however minor, against each of these criteria – major characters must satisfy most or all.

Developing characters develop
This tautology means only that a character (unless a mere walk-on) who can be instantly presented, as Athena from the helmet of Zeus, is quite likely to fall as flat as a board and be as interesting. In real life, who is more boring than the person you meet at a party who spends ten minutes telling you all about himself and then has nothing interesting left to say? So, reveal your

fictional character slowly and preferably in relevant action rather than holding up action merely to describe the character. If you can still be peeling the onion of personality in the very last line, so much the better. Character in this sense is a fine tension building device.

Developing characters are complete
John Braine (p. 132 of *Writing a Novel*) defines the well-made novel as one which leaves no question unanswered in the reader's mind; the same is true of characters. There is no paradox in developing characters also being complete. We are not discussing a fixed point in time but the shifting perception of the character by the reader at any sequential point in the narrative, a compound of the reader having been told everything he could reasonably expect to be told about the character, and the resulting rational expectation that anything relevant *will* in due course be imparted by the author.

Developing characters are internally consistent
All the parts of the whole must gel. This is not a difficult requirement to meet; the danger lies in exceeding it and creating a stereotype or caricature. A Colonel Blimp is a lot easier to paint on the page than a 'neutral' retired army officer. Fortunately, another facet of the developing character almost always saves the thoughtful novice writer.

Developing characters have quirks
This is unpredictability rather than inconsistency. If a character astounds by doing something unmotivated, you will lose your reader's faith in your ability to present a complete, consistent character. If your character surprises and delights the reader with an unpredicted trait, you have fixed your character on the reader's mind as if with photographic chemicals. An example: in *Reverse Negative* the first-person narrator is an elderly bachelor, neat to the point of fussiness (he knows his house was searched because the blankets on his bed are now tucked in at the sides before the bottom), pedantic, patriotic, finicky (he has spent his whole life on twentieth-century British history), sarcastic to anyone who speaks imprecisely, and so on. Yet, while assassins shoot at him, this sedentary scholar tarries to rescue his cat. The

cat made the book for many people. I know this from letters I received from readers and from the fact that some critics who were otherwise repelled by the deliberately cold tone of much of the book (as I've described, half of it was supposed to be written by a computer) mentioned the cat; virtually all the favourable reviewers also seemed keen on the cat. Frankly, I'm no T. S. Eliot or Derek Tangye (I freely admit a preference for dogs), so it is safe to assume that my cat is no better, nor any worse, than your cat or anyone else's cat; what made this cat notable was not the cat itself, but that this almost stereotype dried-up don cherished it. And, because of his love for his cat, he stood out from the crowd of everyone else's dried-up dons and became memorable. Note that there is nothing caricatured or eccentric here: the English are known to be animal-lovers; if he had been a dried-up French don, I would not have given him a cat.

The developing character reverberates

This refers to the character's relationship to the world and people beyond the narrow slice of his life-at-crisis-point you are presenting to the reader. I found out about this by a combination of circumstances: I wanted to write a big novel about the arts in Australia and had a first draft of about 250,000 words. However, my American publishers hated the idea of a novel about the arts and, worse, set in Australia; my London publishers bribed me by commissioning two other novels for about six times what they said they would pay for the arts novel; my Australian publishers offered me as much as they could afford, which would not have paid household expenses while I wrote the book; the Australian Literature Board declined to give me a grant to make up the difference. Then my London paperback publishers built a big warehouse in Australia and, to have something to distribute through it (this is all true), offered to finance the novel if I could deliver quickly and would confine the plot to the thriller sub-plot I had mentioned over lunch (they didn't have time to read the big draft). Reducing 250,000 words to 80,000 produced a novel in which the characters almost seem to glow with undercurrents of past history and associations, sparking off each other like a telephone exchange. (I'm indebted to the freelance editor Shirley Young for the apt phrase 'reverberation' and for pointing out the cause of the

phenomenon.) But not every novel suffers such a chain of fortuitous misfortune and it would be malicious to suggest you over-
write and then cut because mere over-writing, to fill the space,
is not the same as writing a long novel with all the events motivated and then extracting a sub-plot for publication. But, ever
since I found out about reverberation and had its benefit confirmed when I cut another novel from 125,000 to 70,000 words,
I have been consciously providing my characters with a life
beyond what I write down, with a past, with friends the reader
need never hear about, whatever would fill the character out in
real life, away from the present consuming crisis. I do not write
down these perspectives-exterior-to-the-novel (not only a waste
of time but too rigid) but let them illuminate each action in my
mind as I work out the character's story on paper.

Developing characters enjoy life after death
At the end of the novel, the characters will disappear back onto
the library shelf. It is a small, literary death. And that is exactly
what you want your readers to feel, that they have suffered the
loss of old friends. This cannot be done if readers feel they have
exhausted the potential of the characters (has-beens are a bore).
Thus the reader must feel there is an unexplored corner of the
character he wants to know more about; this is not the same as
an unanswered question, more a vague feeling that it would be
good to have the characters around a while longer. Of course,
the characters' other-life reverberations contribute to this, and
so does the strength of character of the leading actors, but a little
sleight of plot can also help, as we shall see at the end of the
next chapter.

Developing characters change
No matter that it doesn't happen often in real life, this is one of
the conventions of literature and the thriller can claim no
exemption; novels are in any event records of the exceptional.
The change need not be large, but it must be consistent with
character and also the magnitude of events – film jargon has it
that the reaction must be 'established' by prior events arranged
in a chain of motivation. In the superior thriller, reactions are
likely to be both subtle and subtly presented by the author. As
an example subtle enough to make the point but not so delicate

as to be elusive, take the culmination of Smiley's *Quest for Karla*, where Smiley takes delivery of Karla at the Berlin Wall. We know Karla has been forced to defect through love of his daughter and we may feel sorry for him. But eyes on Smiley: Karla drops the lighter which he stole from Smiley thirty years ago. The lighter had been a gift to Smiley from his unfaithful wife and is a symbol of the manipulations and humiliations he has suffered from Karla through his puppets, the traitors. The gesture is both Karla's admission of defeat and his statement of defiance. *But Smiley does not pick up the lighter.* This is his acceptance of a pyrrhic victory, his rejection (at last! we've been suffering the bloody woman for over a thousand pages) of his faithless wife, and – in the very closing lines of the novel series – it is Smiley's valedictory. It leaves us indescribably sad because we know there is nothing left for him to do except die. Here, at nearly seventy, Smiley takes, in a few paragraphs, new directions; this culmination is the reader's reward for staying with the character.

Emotional catharsis is, of course, not the only reward the reader may be offered: you may choose to confirm his prejudices, relieve his anxieties, strengthen his faith in the status quo, induce him to re-examine his most fundamental beliefs, whatever – but change is expected and must be provided. The only exception is when the very point of the novel is that *nothing has changed*. This is very tricky to put over convincingly even if you can find a valid example (which would not include the hero failing tragically to achieve his aims, for this is a point of another kind).

Dialogue, action and description

Nabokov said ad nauseam that he considered writers who use more than a page of dialogue at a time to be lazy sods and would therefore not read their novels. This kind of snobbery is a trap into which many new writers and some of the slower critics regularly fall. There is no workable prescriptive theory apportioning the space you should allocate to static description, dialogue and action. Dianne Doubtfire in *Teach Yourself Creative Writing* advocates a third each for dialogue, action and introspection! I find this and other similar advice tends to mechanize art and suggest that instead, without thinking about it too much, you let the story tell itself in the manner that will put it over most effectively.

Defining our terms

Static description is the author telling the reader what a place or object or person looks like; static description is also the author *telling* the reader the salient characteristics of the character. The trouble with such description is proving that it is irrelevant, especially if it is well written, which accounts for so much of the flatulent description which obscures the true thread even in many good novels. Dialogue is what the characters say to each other and to themselves (strictly speaking, interior monologue) and reveals character and furthers the action; empty talk is easy to spot and cut. Action is a mixture of dialogue and description distinguished by the forward momentum of the event being played out. We have already decided that characters are best developed in action rather than through static description.

It would be self-defeating to write 'Joey was apolitical' when you could instead have him say, 'I make bombs for fun, man,' which tells you much more about Joey than merely his lack of interest in politics, builds his character in the reader's mind by the chosen vocabulary, still takes up only the same single line of text (publishers' word counts reckon a short line of text as if it were a full line) and, not least of all, is both more interesting and more convincing for the reader than your blunt say-so.

There are dissenting schools of thought but it seems to me that the modern novel, and in particular the thriller, is less bogged down with static description than previously. By now it should be no secret that I consider this new, leaner aspect of the thriller a good thing. If you want to buck the trend, be sure you have a reason good enough to persuade a publisher.

Dialogue

The primary test for good dialogue is that it must lend itself to reading aloud, and a great many novelists speak their dialogue as they write it. This does not mean that you can tape-record and transcribe everyday conversations: they contain too many pauses, repetitions, irrelevancies and incomplete sentences. You learn to write good dialogue not by listening to people talk but by reading persuasive authors and practising at your keyboard.

The next test you apply, once the dialogue 'scans', is whether you can distinguish the 'voices' of your characters: does each character have his own vocabulary and rhythm of speech? (One way I differentiate my characters is by asking about each one, 'What does this character fear most of all?' Somehow, if I know what he fears, I know how he speaks. I can't guarantee the method but it may work for you as well.) One easy way to differentiate characters' dialogue is to have one person who always speaks precisely and to the point, another who uses circumlocutions and yet another who waffles – but only if it suits the characters you have already developed. If a character stammers, say so, show his handicap once in action, then write his dialogue as if he has no handicap. Similarly, don't let a garrulous character bore the reader; show him in full flow once, then, unless you can use his failing to prolong the tension, summarize what he said ('...but Bill no longer listened to the tale of all John's conquests.') Don't try to render a foreigner's speech phonetically: his vocabulary, sentence construction, speech rhythm and the odd outright error (don't overdo it) will set him apart far more efficiently. In action, dialogue should have a shorter beat than in the more restful scenes. Use the description 'he said' and 'she said' or 'Jack said' rather than tiresomely trying to differentiate each speech; when you do then have cause to write 'Jack shouted angrily', the reader will also have cause to notice.

Dialect writing

Don't. Many registered library-card holders refuse even to attempt dialect books, several paperback publishers have a definite veto on them and, if these commercial considerations aren't enough, dialect destroys the pace of a thriller while the reader tries to decipher your character's message. Read Leo Rosten's introduction to the collected *Kaplan* stories for an expert's view on dialect. If you want to see how dialect can be suggested by vocabulary and rhythm, turn to the master and refresh your memory about James Joyce's Irish in *Ulysses*. Or read Jon Cleary's *A Very Private War*, where he never lets the reader forget that the indigenes speak pidgin yet offers only three actual examples.

5. Plot as Electrified Jigsaw Puzzle

You have your *idea*, you've worked out your *characters* and seen how much of the *plot* follows from characterization. Now, in the *detailed plotting*, we will move the characters from the beginning of the tale to its end, a process the Secker & Warburg editorial director John Blackwell once described as 'fishtailing asymptotically from conception through consumption in the final conflagration'.

Though, for the sake of clarity, we're discussing these concepts (idea, characters/character-generated plot, detailed plotting) separately, it will become obvious when you do it yourself that in fact they all progress simultaneously, with stops and starts to make adjustments in one for the sake of an advance or advantage in any of the others. Once you've had a little practice, the whole thing will seem to spring full-born from your helmet like Athena: the more you practise, the sooner it will happen. However, the order of importance should always be idea, characters, character-inspired plot, detailed plotting.

Character before plot!

There are two reasons for doing your detailed plotting *after* you have given your characters life. The first is that, as we have seen, plot flows most easily and genuinely from character. The second is that, unless your characters live and breathe on the page, the finest plot in the world will not save your book – and every editor and publisher in the world knows this.

You might ask, 'Why not first work out the plot and then simply people it with characters designed expressly for executing the plot?' The short answer is that it doesn't work. I don't know of any exception. This procedure merely delivers wooden characters to well-deserved ridicule and – because the characters lack credibility – laughable plots. Quite literally, and inescapably, dull characters can only be an argument for applying euthanasia to the whole novel. On the other hand, a dud plot can often be fixed without any tears at all, even in none too-expert hands, while an experienced writer will turn the most unpromising plot into a thing of glittering excitement.

Remember, there are only seven original plots and every editor has seen all the variations on every one of them, but the human character offers infinite possibilities.

For the novice, who can pick fantastic plots out of his newspaper every morning but has difficulty delineating and controlling his characters, this seems a harsh constraint. I assure you it is no such thing, it is in fact Liberation Day, as you will discover once you're a little more experienced, when characters will come alive in your hands and suggest twists and turns to set the most skeletal plots dancing.

The mastery of this procedural substance-in-order is your entrée to the higher levels of thrillerdom, where the thriller becomes a novel, becomes art, becomes literature. It is worth the effort.

The importance of being plotted

All that said, the plot is still the second most important element of your thriller, because it expresses your *idea* in logical and progressive form and relates your characters to each other while moving them inexorably towards some revelation the reader wants to know about.

In any event, readers expect the thriller to be strongly plotted and that is a good argument to the writer who wants to be published. In addition, a few pieces by Le Carré notwithstanding, the finest works in the thriller field, those which achieve or approach the most elevated standards of the form, are strongly plotted. The novice can do worse than emulate the masters of the craft to which he aspires. In particular, I would recommend the work of Charles McCarry, perhaps the finest thriller writer of recent times, whose thrillers are all exemplary novels, and Richard Condon, who is best described as a novelist whose novels are more often than not thrillers and who has let fresh light into the musty corners of the novel's structure, content and treatment.

Finally, next to breathing characters, editors look for a good command of the plot. If you have something to say and your characters live – and if he has time – the editor will help you with the plot. But if you can get the plot right by yourself – and, let's face it, this should be the easiest part of writing a book – you've demonstrated a certain commitment to craftsmanship that proves you care and are heading for a second and eighth novel...

How much advance plotting?

You will find, as you grow more experienced, that your confidence in elaborating an idea to a plot to a book grows and so reduces your need for notes. To begin with, however, I suggest you do make notes.

What will you put in your notes? At the top, your central concept (the idea around which the book is to be built, then your character descriptions, both already discussed) – and then, what?

Plotting tools

Most writing processes start with what I call the 'you can't get there from here' syndrome. This is the welter of confusion in which you have an idea but don't know where to start. Every time you pick a loose rag-end, you find that it simply raises more questions, so you pick another one, and so on – until you have a nervous breakdown. You need a tool to shortcut this stage.

The event and the concept

These are your major plotting tools. An **event** is something that happens to your character, whether externally or internally, in the real objective world, or subjectively in his mind. Any narrative is made up of a series of events but don't at this stage worry about the order of events. A **concept** is some point you want to make which can be either very specific (tyranny breeds violence) or abstract (religion is a prison). In either case you must devise events to illustrate the points. At the very least your event must establish circumstances which allow your character or you as the narrator to make an observation expressing the concept.

Next you need tools to expand and relate these events, to sort them into a plot, and to help you devise events to illustrate abstract concepts:

Three-by-five into the Ark Write every event and concept you have on a three-by-five card or a strip of paper, then sort them into a sequence.

Goals and objectives You know where you want the book to end – at the point where your theme is explicated in full, right? But it doesn't happen in one fell swoop. You must have in mind intermediate stages, intermediate events, intermediate resolutions. Write them down on strips of paper. Again, don't fall into the error of premature chronology: any order will do for now, the idea being to dig up the maximum number of bones for your skeleton. You can check later whether it has turned out a neanderthal or a dinosaur and make the necessary adjustments to turn it into the whale you are planning.

Raison d'être Write down all your reasons for writing the book, the concepts you want the book to demonstrate. Now use each individual purpose (e.g. 'Demonstrate the unfairness of the Code Napoléon') at the head of a sheet as a prompt to devise some action to make your point. Refer constantly to your character descriptions – they are certain to suggest something each character will do or say.

Climaxes come first Instead of the hassle of actually devising a plot with substance and detail, author Andrew McCoy sometimes writes the final chapter or section – whichever part delineates the finale – of his novel. Knowing where he wants to arrive, he then sits down in front of blank page 1 and continues to write towards his already standing end. The novice will still, I think, have to plot the in-between stages but in much less detail. The great attraction of this method is that the end of a book is almost always easier to write than the beginning: in a thriller it is very often the 'consumption in the conflagration' and in every kind of novel it is the point where all the difficult and hazardous character and plot development is done and the reward for hard work reaped.

I can heartily recommend this as a plotting device. In a very large sense this method makes the 'fishtailing asymptotically' much less chaotic and fraught for the writer because it then becomes merely a matter of winding up the tension and relaxing it again towards a fixed point, which is clearly much easier to understand and execute when the fixed point stands on paper rather than merely in your mind.

Master scenes synopses This is a tool from another medium, film. A movie is created as visual groupings, called master scenes, each complete in itself. Every narrative contains some 'set pieces', usually climaxes and turning points (the battle scenes in Shakespeare), which are easily visualised and described as scenes in a film. If you intend to be a very visual writer, your proposed book will probably roll in front of your mind's eye as pictorial events, mini-acts in a play, which with very little mental effort you can then write down in this compact but very informative format. Here's a sample of a synopsis of a master scene:

31. Interior. Sir Oliver's room. Evening.

Sir Oliver and PM allocate Cabinet posts. Cynicism about abilities and ambitions of colleagues. Generator out. Sir Oliver wants to confront Electricians' Union for blacking Government, but PM is wary.

Key sets Or you might just write down the key events, put them in order and then actually write the key set-pieces, filling in the connecting narrative later.

Formal structures

Usually the formal structuring devices you learn about at school and university are of little use to the working writer but, in a limited number of quite specific cases, they can be helpful.

Beginning, middle and end

You have all your notes but are in a dither of indecision as to where what goes. This condition arises particularly with the realistic, semi-documentary novel which strings almost random events together. However, you are faced with the imperative that your characters develop, and there will certainly be one event that will be more suitable for the last section of the novel than any of the others. It is in instances like this that three piles of notes labelled Beginning, Middle and End, can help. You then use one of the other techniques to sort within each pile.

Thesis, antithesis, synthesis

A structure of statement, counter-statement and resolution is an essential tool for the novel of ideas, especially if it is a bit short on action, because it allows interior tension to be set up. It is also a useful tool when the black hats are to be given a turn at the lectern and an entitlement to doubt. Neither of these applications is to be lightly undertaken but with practice you do get it right – it took me forty-odd tries with *Reverse Negative*, but then the theme of this book is that commitment will triumph. The practical problem is that each side must speak in its own voice, which we have already seen is difficult. And 'synthesis' of the two views, in practice finding a resolution without fear or favour for one side or the other, is so fraught that even experienced writers come unstuck. Paradoxically, this format is an easy option when there are no distinct black hats, merely unfortunate circumstances, as in many disaster novels (I learnt this in writing *Sinkhole*) and in the 'social' thriller. However, if you know Black from White, Good from Evil, and you have no intention of letting the bad guys take over the church, this format merely looks tricksy and smartypants and puts a lot of people off. Also, if the weight of what you have to say doesn't justify the treatment, stay clear or the critics will fry you for a pompous ass.

Spiral of climaxes

This is an academic evergreen and fits any narrative fiction in all of the literary forms. The flow of events is described as an ascending spiral of climaxes, or as a series of build-ups each to its own climax or, rather fancifully, as a climax-anti-climax cycle. Please show me the registered library-card holder who admits to being 'into anti-climaxes'... It all sounds most plausible until you start trying to put a plot on paper in spirals and find you still need to create events, to sort events into an order and to rank events for importance to your narrative, all the time having to take care of characters who get queasy on the swoops and roundabouts and wander off to the hotdog stand. You might be able to handle it but I find it conceptually similar and much simpler to plan the high spots (climaxes) as set pieces and then to plot the sections in between to lead the imagination straight into the climax. Also, I think a series of climaxes is correct and desirable in a thriller but this business of *escalating* climaxes, i.e. each at a higher pitch than the previous one, is a bit like painting-by-numbers and the results impress equally.

The rule, though not inviolable, is that you put your biggest climax at or towards the end of the book. The thriller writer falls naturally into this habit and lets the rest of the climaxes fall where the characters dictate regardless of relative size or any sterile formula.

The John Braine method

I wrote my first novel by this method long before I read John Braine's *Writing a Novel* – and Hemingway hit upon a version before either of us was born – but I found it too circuitous and have since worked out the shortcuts above in the process of writing subsequent novels. However, his own variant here described obviously works for Mr Braine and it could work for you, too. It has the advantage for the novice that he can at once satisfy his burning desire to start writing his novel.

- Once you have your central concept or idea, either make a synopsis of no more than 500 words, or sit straight down to write your first draft. It is useful to have to hand a list of names suitable for your characters so that the flow of words isn't held up while you consult the gazetteer but you should give your characters no further conscious thought because 'they will reveal themselves in their actions.' (Braine, ibid., p. 21)

- You write this first draft at white-hot speed, never missing a scheduled writing session and writing the maximum number of words at each session. Don't hold up the flow of words to worry about details – make notes in the margin to research or invent such details at a later stage. All that is important is to finish the first draft as quickly as possible. Don't check back, don't revise, just write to that target (80,000 words is good). The sense of achievement you will experience on finishing the first draft is indescribable; savour it, because it comes only once at such intensity.

- Now, make a *prose* summary of the novel, in no more than 2000 words, from which a clear chain of motivation unifying the whole narrative should be discernible before you pass to the next step. Braine suggests you might achieve this 'organic unity' in six tries at rewriting the outline; if it takes more, I suggest you go on to the next step all the same because it is amazing how many planning problems disappear when you stop writing mere dead notes and start writing the novel.

- The next step is a formal plot structure broken down sequentially event by event into chapters (or whatever narrative units you choose). All events must be time-specific and by now you should know both the period the novel is set in and the amount of 'real' time the action covers (anything from a few hours to a year – don't try for a bigger chunk of time in your first novel).

- Now write down the names of your characters and their salient characteristics as briefly as possible as described in the previous chapter.

- Check for libel.

- Do the minimum of essential research (see chapter on research); buy (or photocopy at the library – even small libraries have map departments hidden at the back) maps and street plans of all the places you intend using, or draw your own if you are inventing the setting.

- The final task before you start writing the second draft is to determine the 'tone of voice' (Norman Podhoretz, *Making It*) in which you will write. My experience is that first novelists know the tone of voice they want (even if they choose the wrong tone) and that this block is more likely to hinder the writer's second and subsequent works. Braine advises you not to panic, to sit quietly and think about your characters meeting the reader. But that is a counsel of perfection from a highly disciplined professional writer. Shameful though the confession is, the first time I was faced with it, I used the search for the right tone of voice as an excuse to put off starting the huge task of the second draft. If you choose this method, on no account must more than a week pass before you start work on the second draft; if, after a week, you do not have the right tone of voice, start writing all the same. If what you write is terrible, keep going until it improves: *that* will be the right tone of voice. Now scrap what you have written and start at the beginning again with that tone of voice.

- The paramount rule is, again, not to let anything interfere with the forward flow of your novel, never to miss a writing session for any reason. However, in the beginning, the second draft will progress much more slowly than the first but, towards the end, you will have to resist the temptation to hurry to see it finished and should make a conscious effort to slow yourself down so that your ending is perfect.

- Do not reread or polish until you have finished this draft.

If you choose this method, you should definitely read Mr Braine's much fuller description (pp 20–34 in *Writing a Novel*) and pay particular attention to the chapter in which I deal with writers' blocks because the method is fraught with them.

You choose among these procedures, informal or formal, by the dictates of your material and your experience. You can mix and match methods by trial and error even within one book.

Too much plotting

There is such a thing as too much plotting. I've had several books aborted at the conceptual stage simply because an editor wanted to know in too much detail what I intended to say. In bringing enough order to the ideas in my mind to speak or write intelligently about them at 'sales director length', I plumbed all their mysteries and, since there was nothing more to discover in the actual writing, lost my enthusiasm. I should have told these editors where to get off but didn't then know of the dire consequences to follow.

It is therefore well to leave yourself much to discover in the plot that will occur to you as you write it, some small delight to turn every day at your typewriter into a joyous journey of exploration instead of drudgery 'by the letter of the plot'. Remember, what you will eventually publish is not the perfect outline but a novel that should be as fresh and enthusiastic as you can make it, and you can't do that by numbers, even if you marked up the numbers yourself.

Unfortunately, this is a counsel of perfection. It is now difficult even for established writers and almost impossible for novices to be published without making extensive outlines. In the 1980s and 1990s our profession suffered (a carefully chosen word) a radical change. Previously a large minority of publishers demanded a synopsis and a sample chapter or three; the substantial majority would read full manuscripts arriving unsolicited from aspirants, and knew their established authors well enough to trust them to develop a full plot from an outline of a maximum of, say, 2000 words. Most of my own novels were commissioned from a single paragraph on a sheet of paper which a commissioning editor waved around in a meeting with in his other hand one of my paperbacks with on the cover 'bestselling author of...' to persuade Doubting Thomases. Those days are gone forever.

Now the majority of publishing houses will not accept full manuscripts but instead demand a synopsis and sample chapters from aspirants and professionals alike. (It is also wise to send a synopsis even when a full manuscript is offered, but that answers a different problem.) The temptation in these circumstances is, of course, to write only the sample chapter(s) and the synopsis on the assumption that it makes more sense to complete only those books that actually interest a publisher. The difficulty is that the assumption on the part of the publisher is that you, the author, will tell him everything relevant in the synopsis – and that is an opportunity to lose all your enthusiasm for the project. What I and many others used to consider substantial and substantive outlines are now widely regarded by editors (especially Americans) as merely a base on which to open a dialogue which usually arrives in the form of an irresistible request for expansive explication.

This practice is now so prevalent and so unlikely to be reversed, and has already had such serious and widespread repercussions for the vast majority of writers, that I have been asked by a publisher to write a book on the remedies, with the predictable title of *Writing Proposals and Synopses That Sell*. Kenneth Atchity's book on treatments for film actually featured on the bestseller list published by the Los Angeles *Times*.

Recently, for a proposed series of five to seven lightweight adventures, a New York editor in the end had 50,000 words of plot and samples out of me – half the wordage of one of the projected books! – before I decided the project had died under its own bloated weight and walked away at precisely the moment he put his firm's money on the table. It would have been dishonest to accept commissions for books I had come to hate fervently.

Novices are well advised to write the whole book before making a detailed synopsis and choosing sample chapters to offer. Any other process is simply too destructive of essential spontaneity.

Professional writers must make their own arrangements. For myself, having gone briefly with the flow to test its worth, I shall in future tell editors demanding extended outlines to take the entrepreneurial risks – judging the monetary value of authors and projects – for which they are paid fat salaries.

The demand for extended outlines is one of the reasons why established professionals, who could if they wish have their novels commissioned, prefer to write the book first and to sell it only when it is complete. They, of course, have the advantage over aspirants that publishers are keen to accept their complete manuscripts and will read them attentively.

Too much plot

The absolute novice, struggling to define enough events to express his idea at novel-length, may find this hard to believe, but having too much plot is an affliction that strikes the new writer, writing his first or second or third manuscript, rather than the experienced writer. The practised writer will save some of the events for another book, the aspirant tries to cram in every event he can think of – and disaster strikes! What happens is that characters don't have breathing room to develop because they are in action without pause for thought every moment they are on stage. Uni-dimensional characters result and the plot (which might be excellent if only there were less of it) becomes ludicrous. In addition, the reader becomes a spot breathless because there is no time between the climaxes to recover and prepare for the next one.

Critics often damn the resulting thrillers as 'comic books' but the real culprit is probably the police-procedural teleseries with which a whole generation of writers has now grown up. However, the reader of a book makes a conscious commitment by *choosing* your book from a very wide selection, while the television viewer takes what he gets or is offered only a limited choice. The experience of reading a book being so much more intense than watching television, the reader probably *needs* breathing spaces.

Finally, you might consider that the reader invests effort in your book because he hungers for something television doesn't satisfy – and, since television is heavily plotted, your edge is in more sensitive character handling and development, for which television does not have time but for which you can easily make space by pruning your plot.

Of course, I'm not making an argument for the lightweight plot. Thrillers by definition have strong plots. But a point will arise when you will have to ask yourself if you really need the twenty odd major events you have plotted to explicate your idea; won't ten do as well and result in a stronger novel because your characters will have space to develop and grow?

How many events – or, more precisely, groups of events each leading to a climax – do you need? As many as will put over your idea through the actions of your characters. An Eng Lit postgrad student told me my novels – generally thought to be heavily plotted – usually have ten to fifteen 'action-reaction cycles' compared to five or six in a Le Carré novel. But the number-count depends too much on definition of 'a cycle', the magnitude of climax one recognizes and extraneous factors to be of much help to you; such an analysis is also intrinsically misleading because it invites comparison of apples and oranges. My best advice to you is to write the narrative for all the events that you have planned and then to see which you can cut or combine without harm to the whole. That way you soon build up a feeling for what contributes and what merely occupies space.

Start writing now

Thrillers come in all shapes and sizes and convolutions; they are distinguished from other narratives not by format but by a greater endowment of tension. Aspirants are sometimes told that the thriller writer *plots* for tension but that advice does him great disservice. You cannot plan or plot for tension, you *write* for tension. A plot is merely a sequence of events selected to illustrate some concept or idea you have. True, the order of events have a certain inherent edge-of-the-chair potential but that is all it is, until you realize the potential on the page.

Tension is a function of the reader's identification with the character in jeopardy – to state the obvious, you must present the character for that identification before the reader will thrill to his danger. I shall therefore assume, in the discussion of the tension building methods and devices, that you have sorted your notes and perhaps retyped them and are now in the process of writing your novel, stopping every so often to turn to me for help because you feel the tension lagging.

Jeopardy and double jeopardy

These are *The Perils of Pauline*, the villain gaining the upper hand, the heroine an inch from imaginative death if the hero doesn't extract digit pretty pronto. In our subtler times we pretend to arrange things with a little more finesse but the principle is the same and arises naturally from the two sets of characters you've chosen to create and the situations you place them in – or, if you've done your work well, they place themselves in by the friction between them. Your detailed plot should, I think, do little more than provide for the collision of opposites, leaving you to create the ensuing results in the actual writing.

It's easy to go over the top with jeopardy, double and triple jeopardy. Modern readers, educated well beyond the Bulldog Drummond kneejerk school of thrillers, will accept much subtler plots than even a decade ago. More to the point, they will reject anything that isn't realistically possible or, at best, read it as a comic send-up. However, so much that once seemed improbable now gets reported as hard news that even over-the-top plots may be overtaken by real life between writing and publication day.

Start with a bang

Yes, I know, one works up to a climax. But, in the real world, the writer has to convince a publisher's reader, then an editor, then the publisher (who tells the editor whether and how much money to offer you) – all of whom are likely to make up their minds after reading *only ten pages or less* of the manuscript you have slaved over for months, perhaps years. Even if you pass 'go' with them, they won't buy your second book if the first one doesn't sell. Your book will sell in hardcover to librarians and in paperback to book buyers. They may decide to buy after reading only the first page or even paragraph.

What if opening with a bang doesn't suit your story? Then I suggest, unless you are superbly confident, you change the story. And if you can't change the story, *add* something. *The Zaharoff Commission*, when I completed the first draft, started with a meeting between Basil Zaharoff, Lloyd George and Georges Clemenceau, an impressive piece of historical reconstruction but still just three men sitting round a table talking. It was what I had promised the two publishers who commissioned the novel but I felt unhappy about the slow start. The novel could not be restructured to put later action first but there was a remark about events that had occurred before the time-span of the novel, so I wrote two prologues and they not only provided *two* bangs but strengthened the book immensely by providing further motivation for the main action. Andrew McCoy wrote *African Revenge* as a tale of crocodile hunting in Africa and discovered, only days before the delivery deadline, that by giving the young hero, as a reason for joining the dangerous safari, only the single line, 'What they threatened to do to me if I didn't pay is worse than death,' he had thrown away an opportunity. He rectified this, not by expanding the line, which after all only *tells* what happened, but by writing an opening section set in a gambling den to *show* why Lance had no option but to run. Look to any later stages of your novel that you have already written (or carry in your mind) for a suggestion about an opening with a whiff of gunpowder, or look to your character descriptions for something out of their pasts that you can use. Almost always writing such a section to open the book after you've 'finished', as distinct from and in addition to rewriting the original opening pages, will turn out to be a good move. You will be more familiar with the characters and more confident of your skill in manipulating them, and the reader will immediately see them full-blown in action.

If nothing else avails, offer the reader as an opening bang a preview of your dénouement. Films sometimes do this behind the main title sequence. Andrew McCoy, having experienced the advantage of this method once, says, '*The Meyersco Helix* in the first draft opened with middle-class people talking about rare moles – the kind that dig up your lawn – and having sex. Hardly a gripper for a novel in which an American president ends up nuking Boston. I didn't hesitate a second. I decided the original opening was commonplace but unavoidable, and in the next moment I hit the keys to tell how the President was woken and told he had two minutes to decide whether he wanted to nuke Boston or face having the entire nation killed by a virulent disease. That set an entirely different, violently urgent tone right from the beginning.'

Books, parts, chapters, sections

Within days of starting to write a thriller you will be faced with a problem which is simultaneously an opportunity.

The problem is this: where do you put the breaks? And, what kind of breaks do you need or want? There are all kinds of theories about this but a perennial bestselling author puts them in perspective: 'I write from nine in the morning till five in the afternoon, when I close the chapter and open the bar.' Just like that. She has the experience and the skill never to keep the punctual guest waiting for his sherry. But there is no law which says you have to write in chapters, of whatever length. You could choose to break, instead, each time your characters leave one country for another, each time a new character is introduced, whenever a climax is done, just before every climax. Your choice of break indicators is equally varied, from mere line spaces to parts with their own part-titles on otherwise virgin right-hand pages.

Many novices follow the example of their peers and split the narrative into near-equal length chapters virtually at random. Such peers are not necessarily betters, especially where slavish emulation leads the aspirant to miss an opportunity. Chapters are a device left over from the prehistory of the modern novel, when books were read aloud in country houses – and later published in monthly instalments in magazines – and it was incumbent on the author to cut such lengths of narrative cloth as could conveniently be read aloud in an evening. The modern writer, who knows he need take no account of the vocal chords of his reader, misses a golden opportunity to put the formal breaks of the narrative to productive use when he merely chops his story into chapters like so many lengths of salami. These breaks can be chosen and staggered to vary the pace and rhythm of your tale, to heighten the suspense, to signal your intent to the reader, and probably other useful purposes you can think up if you put your mind to it.

Writing tension

Characters, as we saw in earlier chapters, create tension; the events that make up the plot have the potential for tension; the narrative form you choose and the natural breaks of the story offer further potential for building tension. But the essential element of 'unputdownability' is created line by line, from the very first line.

Starts

The importance of the first page has already been alluded to but the opening line of every new section is equally important. A 'section' is here defined as any part of the narrative divided from the rest in any manner whatsoever, even if merely by a line space which may or may not contain an asterisk or violin hole. It is a natural break and a place at which the reader may be tempted to put down your book. You have twelve, at most sixteen, words to hook him into reading on, or to leave him eager to return to your book at the earliest possible moment to find out what happens next.

Meanwhile back at the ranch...

That's perhaps the most famous top-of-the-form hook of them all and absolutely archetypal. The purpose is to pique your reader's curiosity. At all but the first section, your reader will already be involved with your characters and will want to know what happens next. In addition, he reads your *thriller* in the expectation of being thrilled – and nothing thrills like tension. He has a right not to be let down and if you do let him down

too often he will put your book down. One of the most effective ways of giving the reader value for his money is through
'hooks'. These are carefully crafted sentences at the beginning
and end of every section that warn him that more thrilling
events are about to happen to his favourite characters. Here are
a few samples from *Sinkhole*:

In the end, oil killed an American city.

10.33 a.m. 'Praise the Lord for booze and pass the bottle.'

11.19 a.m. 'Oh Paul, you shouldn't!'

11.46 a.m. 'Sweetass!'

12.06 p.m. Altogether the most fearful thing was the roaring,
grinding groan of earth tearing earth, rock gnashing against
rock like the teeth of an angry dragon.

12.06 p.m. For the first time in her life she regretted her
agnosticism.

Most of these lines are short, but not many readers are likely to
stop reading the longer sample after their eye has caught 'most
fearful'. Each of these samples (taken at random from near the
beginning of the book) and the others that open sections are
designed to make the reader ask *who? why? when? what? how?*
and to let his curiosity lead him into the next section. This is a
very important technique for all writers but for thriller writers
it is indispensable. One of these sentences is at the end of a section – 'In the end, oil killed an American city.' – and serves to
give warning of what is to happen: in a sense it promises the
reader great excitement if he will stay with the narrative through
the exposition that follows until the action picks up again.

'To Harry Maxim it seemed as if his wife died twice.' After
such an opening line, which reader could bear to put down Gavin
Lyall's *The Secret Servant* without finding out more about Harry
Maxim?

This technique has fringe benefits. You will find that consideration of the opening sentence of each section forces you to
review very closely and to order in your mind the events in that
section, and also to decide how you want the characters to
develop through those events.

Breaks

Besides the formal breaks of chapters or sections, there are also logical dramatic breaks in any extended narrative. I have already made a case that on commercial grounds your dramatic breaks should coincide with your formal breaks, but you can use your breaks to great dramatic effect to build tension, sometimes simply by inserting a break when the reader already knows action is imminent. Then you may continue in the new section where you left off in the old (don't overdo it, though), but more often it is worth changing viewpoints or interposing something else to drag the suspense out a little longer.

Rhythm

Your characters and, through them, your plot will impose a certain rhythm on your narrative. Your breaks can help and your language should quicken towards the end of the story. You will probably find a rhythmic cycle of description, dialogue and action, of long passages and short, of languid language and blunt. But I've never heard of any but the pseuds *planning* for this except in the very largest sense of knowing it is available to the diligent practitioner and determining that they would work hard to achieve it in their own books.

Though you may not consciously be able to plan for good rhythm, you can and should watch out even at the planning stage for bad rhythm, which is generally mechanical, obvious rhythm. Avoid sections of absolutely regular length, or regularly alternating length, or writing point and counterpoint iteration like a marital squabble in a soap opera.

You can study rhythm in other writers' successful books but the best teacher is practice at your keyboard.

Flashbacks

If you intend using a flashback to heighten tension, you should first be absolutely certain that it is relevant and also that it is relevant *at that point*: if the reader can see a better place for it without even trying, he will know you for a trickster. Besides the obvious informative, motivational and tension-enhancing aspects of the flashback, I should like to recommend the device as a narrative technique with an almost automatic near-mesmeric rhythm. The master of the flashback is, beyond any shadow of doubt, Jerome Weidman: his *The Sound of Bow Bells* is written almost entirely in flashback with – wait for it – nested mini-flashbacks. But don't be misled by Mr Weidman's apparent ease, it is a very difficult technique to handle convincingly without much experience and practice.

The fugue

This is a term used by television directors (and mispronounced 'few-gew' by them despite the best educational efforts of the writers) to indicate a carry-over link between adjacent scenes. The most common example is the unseen phone incongruously ringing at the end of one scene and seen to be answered in a completely different location at the beginning of the next scene. Novel writers can use the device to link their scenes – for instance, where something seen triggers off a memory that leads into a flashback.

Symbols that you carry forward as part of a character's psychological baggage may also be used to prepare the reader for the advent of the character a couple of paragraphs before he actually appears. Or you can use recurring images or symbols or minor characters in this method to establish a rhythm or vary the pace.

Another, most imaginative, version of the fugue is the *crash-forward* found in William Goldman's *The Color of Light* where two meetings of children of alcoholic parents are used to skip the story forward several years right in the middle of a paragraph with the shocking mini-dénouement delayed for another few paragraphs. Mr Goldman never does return to tell us what happened in those lost years...

Creative clawback

By now, you may think I'm a kleptomaniac pilferer of tools from other media: computing, economics, psychology for my characters, the films for plotting methods. In fact, they are the ones who've been borrowing techniques wholesale from literature: Freud wrote, in the view of some, *very* imaginative literature. I'm merely recovering what is a fictionalist's birthright. If you see a tool that looks useful, pick it up and use it! Who cares if professors of Eng Lit don't recognize it as a literary artifact? You're writing books to be read while you're alive, not studied after you're dead. Incidentally, there is no copyright on ideas and it would in any event be churlish for a writer who developed a new form to attempt to deny it to others, who may perhaps use it better. If you want to use the computer synthesis device I developed for *Reverse Negative*, feel free, just as I took the device of starting each section in *Sinkhole* with a clock-timing from Richard Martin Stern.

The dénouement

This is where you bring all the threads together, solve the puzzle and zap the baddie with his just deserts while, with the other hand, giving the hero the girl. In the classic detective story, that is. There has never been a requirement for thrillers of a more general nature to tie *all* the ends up neatly and, besides, the perfect happy ending is often unrealistic in the circumstances the modern thriller writer is apt to set up.

However, it helps in writing the book if you plot and write as if you *intend* tying all the ends up neatly. This is not difficult to do once you have the first draft and start rewriting it. Loose ends normally reside in characters who turn out to be superfluous but, if you do not start out with an Agatha Christie frame of mind, the middle portions of the writing are very likely to defeat you.

All of that said, it is far better for the pieces of your jigsaw puzzle at the end to have a realistic fit, even if slightly clumsy (because that is how people are, slightly clumsy), than a too-good but glaringly artificial forced fit.

End with a bang

Even if your biggest climax is for some reason not the last one in the book, thriller readers expect a big climax at or quite near the end of the book. One sometimes hears writers advocate that the reader be given time to wind down gently after the last climax but I don't know that this applies to thrillers. What I have done, and been commended for by the more serious critics, is to include, where my central characters were real persons, appendices of verifiable facts from their lives plus a bibliography so that the interested reader can judge for himself what liberties if any I took with the truth. From their letters, I know that many readers do read these non-fiction addenda, but whether for the purpose of winding down, I can't say. The majority of thriller writers, judging by their work and what they say, fail to be convinced by the 'winding down' argument. Bang and out!

The twist in the tail

This is not a gentle letdown but a secondary, unexpected climax which turns everything the reader has been led to believe on its head. For instance, in my novel *Festival*, the hero, an impresario named Ransome, is drawn into helping his friend the conductor Vlaklos defect to the West under the nose of the cultural commissar Kerensky, also Ransome's friend. Somehow Ransome blunders through – only to discover, after he has endangered his career and life, that Kerensky's task was to harass Vlaklos into defection because the conductor was too famous to incarcerate in a psychiatric institute... When I started writing, I used to regard these 'kickers' in the novels of published writers with great envy, but now I know it is an easier technique than, for instance, the properly placed and controlled flashback. You merely add your second most-favourite ending for the story and then return to plant a few clues to the twist in the tail so that the reader is not cheated, not forgetting at the same time to water down any overly explicit clues because making it too easy for the reader is another no-no.

Tragedy and memorability

The classics owe their memorability in a very large measure to the fact that they are tragedies. If you haven't yet read the great Russians, may I suggest that any writer needs at least passing acquaintance with Dostoievsky, Turgenev, Pasternak and Tolstoi? They will make my point for me. The tragic failure and the good man going down struggling, sympathetically written on a large canvas, is the stuff of Literature with a capital.

Unfortunately the thriller writer can in most instances not kill his hero without cheating his readers most outrageously; the reader has been rooting for that man and, even if the hero cannot win, dare you leave the reader without hope that Good will live to fight another day?

There is also a commercial reason for letting the hero live. Andrew McCoy was told by several serious readers of his novel *The Insurrectionist*, none of them under any illusion that it was anything but a realistic novel of political violence (a phrase which almost defines the modern thriller), that they deeply regretted that he as the writer had seen fit to kill one of the two protagonists (the book doesn't actually have any heroes) *even if he deserved his fate many times over*. Without proposing that *The Insurrectionist* should end any other way, may I suggest that this is part of what made those people remember the book? Next time they're standing in front of a shelf, making their choice, do they say, 'Ah, an Andrew McCoy I haven't read. He's that fearless writer who tells it like it is regardless of consequences,' or will they think, 'That bloody McCoy. In that other book he built me up only to cast me down. It was weeks before I could get the damned thing out of my mind. Never again!'

Nobody but you can decide which is right for you and your books. You certainly can't use a dead hero in a series. But then you may want to be a serious writer who sets people thinking or you may have no fear of coming up with a new set of characters and ideas for each new book.

There is a halfway house. This is the sorrowful but not truly tragic ending. Here the hero survives but his triumph is bought at the price of something he values dearly, perhaps the life of a friend or a girl, or perhaps disillusionment with the ideals that drove him thus far. He, and therefore you, have to take the loss seriously and it has in itself to be credible, otherwise readers will see it as mock-tragedy. Another name for mock-tragedy is comedy: ask Woody Allen. In practice, this balance is so difficult to achieve that, if you must have tragedy, it is often safer to forego the sequel or series and kill the hero. As a consolation, the resulting thriller is more likely to be reviewed as a serious novel by the highbrow critics.

6. Psyche: changes in hero(ine) and audience*

The thriller, taken as a genre, is itself a record of change – in other words, history. Today you would guarantee the return, unread, of a ms by calling it *Ten Little Niggers*, whereas you will at half-a-dozen publishers I can name receive very special attention for a ms titled *Ten Little Lesbians*. In fifty years, you can bet on it, 'lesbians' will be considered namecalling as offensive as 'niggers' is today.

History and contemporary popular culture

We live on the cusp of the changeover between the age of transport, which started with the poet Alexander Pope and is now well past its zenith, and the next great age, that of communication, which is already swinging into action.

The thriller before 1940 was essentially, when it was not a murder mystery, a chase, a race not just against time but literally along a road or across a sea. That worked through into pop art from 1950 onwards: Bruce Springsteen stands at the end of a line, holding hands with the Beach Boys, and so on until at the misty end of vision we are just touching fingers with Henry Ford and Erskine Childers.

Today a common thriller theme somehow involves computers, and persons who can understand and operate them. The person who understands electronics has progressed from being the hero's tagalong nerd to being the hero. Bill Gates of Microsoft is the richest man in the world.

*This is a chapter intended for advanced writers, with several thrillers completed, perhaps even published, who have gained enough in craftsmanship and confidence to tackle substantially more difficult projects. The novice is advised to skip this chapter for now or to read it for interest while following the proven guides in the rest of this book.

In between we had a mini-nuclear age, in which the characters were those who commanded or understood hydrogen explosions and the missiles to deliver them. That was such a rich vein it will run for another half-century; if you doubt the forecast, ask yourself how long since Hitler's thousand-year reich ended in tears, and point to any year since then which didn't have at least one big seller based on the Nazis' wrongdoings. As I write this at the second edition (1994), the current 'Nazi bestseller', available even in my small Irish village, is by Robert Harris. Five years later at the third edition (early 1999 as I write this), my current reading is the new Jack Higgins bestseller, *Flight of Eagles*.

In Pope's time the popular hero was the learned and witty Dr Johnson; the contemporary chattering classes would have set their dogs on the unshaven Springsteen and all the other professional proletarians who so miraculously manage a day-old beard every day of their lives. Today there are those who would like to bring back Joe Stalin and Dr Strangelove because with Mutual Assured Destruction (MAD) at least everyone knew where they stood and all the big boys were against the little psychopaths. These are precisely the same people who would condemn your thriller out of hand, in the unlikely event that you succeed in having it published, if your hero were a Bulldog Drummond stereotype.

History and the hero
What can we conclude from this jumble of odd historical but umbilically connected facts and opinions?

Forget for the moment the obvious conclusion, that a writer has a very odd mind, best illustrated by the image of horror-writer Stephen King from his porch in small-town America asking the passing doctor, already suspicious of this apparently idle Bohemian, how one would go about strangling a cat. And forget, above all other distractions, that if I had a whole chapter or a book to expand the bald notes above, it would probably make an impressive socio-historic document; we deal elsewhere with history as history, and history as insight.

Concentrate instead on the people in this rush through the centuries, and *how the popular image of those we would most like to emulate has changed*. Take a break: think really hard about this concept, especially if it is novel to you.

What's in it for you?

This is essentially another way of looking at character. These are not yet your own characters but they are characters that consumers of culture (including readers) demonstrably find easy to identify with. Therefore you should be able to learn something from them which may enhance your own work and chances of finding an audience, which in this book we are equating with publication.

At the crudest level, if you seek a central concept and character, choosing someone in one of the modern iconic professions, such as a pop star, will at the very least permit you the possibility of cross-genre sales with glitz, because you will be appealing to the prurient interests of the peeping toms who are fascinated by how the rich and immoral live. Keep in mind that this desire in a large part must have motivated the sales of those inspirational novels which showed us the dissolute Romans or Victorian fallen women about their sinful business before proceeding to how they were saved by faith alone. Melvyn Bragg, slightly less crudely, chose a television executive as the central character for one of his books – the principle is the same.

Psyche: the imperative of change

Two points arise from these considerations. One is that the modern hero, because he is in flux between fixed moralities, needs far less character-building to be interesting than heroes of earlier times; this is, of course, to the advantage of the thriller writer, who must always keep his eye on the pace of his story. It is not even necessary to assume that another fixed morality will triumph, say, when the Muslims conquer the world, but the flux towards an unknown is equally frightening.

In addition, the difficulties caused by the literary presumption of change in characters as a precondition of narrative success are decreased because so much uncertainty and change are inherent in any realistic environment that the character's reaction to pre-existing external events builds character.

Neither item is much of a free lunch, because these benefits are the result of circumstances that in a single generation have increased by several magnitudes the skills required from thriller-writers for entry to and survival in the profession. Uncertainty and flux are in themselves not easy narrative material for novices.

Becoming a prophet

You can do more than passively flow with the tide. You can gather in these changing perceptions – and desires – from society at large and use them to elevate your thrillers into the highest literary class.

Consider the high literary view that books lead the way, that writers, including the best novelists, provide a moral interpretation that the rest may live by. This is a valid view – large parts of the Christian and Muslim and especially the Indian holy books are creative narrative writing of a very high order – but it is possible that it is less valid in our time than in Nietzsche's a century ago simply because our philosophers have abdicated the search for truth in their cowardly retreat towards philology (jargon for semantics). Since then it seems at least likely that, instead of percolating ideas downwards from elevated thinkers, novelists have been originating these ideas, putting them into the popular culture, and watching them bubble upward towards the sort of 'thinker' who tells us the definition of good is the lowest common denominator. From the pop philosophers worthwhile ideas eventually percolate towards such serious thinkers as have not been seduced by television.

This analysis, if even partially correct, puts you, the writer, in the driving seat of our society. A bishop, whom I have not known to voice an exaggeration in twenty years, admits in private that John Grisham's thriller about the lawyer fallen among the indigent will do more for poor relief fundraising than all the bishops' combined preaching from their pulpits.

Compare Lillian Hellman's *The Little Foxes* with Frank Yerby's *The Foxes of Harrow*. Let us be clear, I'd rather read Yerby than Hellman any day of the year. But the important story, because it made lesbianism an acceptable subject for popular culture, is Hellman's. She also created the lesbian heroine and laid a foundation stone of one wing of the feminist movement.

Hellman is a literary prophet.

Of course, it will not be given to all of us, or even to many, to mark the change in literature and life quite so sharply.

But even at a much lower level there are huge harvests waiting to be reaped by the writer who keeps his eyes open for what people do, his ear to the pulse of history and his mouth shut until he has something to say. A detective with AIDS might not make for a long-lived series, but the very urgency which attends every act of his own limited life would carry over into his work and so make him an extremely interesting character in any kind of fiction and, of course, particularly in a thriller, where tension and pace are so important. If you then succeed in making your book say something universal about AIDS, that would be literature and, if your statement were pointed and different and relevant enough, you, too, would become a prophet.

What makes the spurt of novels after any major war so striking is that they, all at once, celebrate, forecast and shape a radically new society in the instant that it comes into existence.

The longest peace

Ours has been the most peaceful century ever. Its wars, to be certain, left millions dead, but in the perspective of history they were short, sharp and to the point. Tyrants have killed more of their own citizens in this century, in Germany and Russia and 'democratic' Kampuchea (Cambodia) and China, than wars ever did.

Thus, when I wanted to know why throughout this century we have betrayed our dreams when the means for their realization lay readily to hand (this is also the richest century, and its people the longest lived, in all history), I did not in the first instance consider the crisis points of the major wars. No, I went straight for the practitioners of intelligence, who are by definition patriots and who, among those I have met, included some of the most intelligent, thoughtful and moral men of their nations. At this point it was clear, to me if not to the publisher I persuaded to commission the trilogy of novels about intelligence in our century in which I intended to work out this question, that the Russian empire would break up and that soon afterwards the people would turn on the KGB and destroy it.* The historical spread of 'in our century' would give me the scope

---

*It may be more precise to say that the publisher didn't think the destruction or otherwise of the KGB relevant to the success of the narratives he was paying for. It is of course true that the threat of destruction of institutions is often a greater catalyst than the actual event, because a threat may be countered while reconstruction after the event may be impossible.

to ask how the intelligence agent has changed over time, and what forces impelled the change. I chose to tell my story as a saga of linked families and in the form of a thriller; obviously, within a length for the complete trilogy of 750,000 words and a timespan of 75 years, several mini-thrillers will happen. The larger thriller is the survival of families, of nation-states, of contrasting ideologies, of the good that is in all of us.

Note that it is implicit in all this that neither the commissioning publisher nor I believe that in a properly written novel it matters that historically the outcome is known. Readers want to know how and why it happened, and in any event their focus after a few pages is on the characters, after which the writer can shape history as his experience and personal authority permit. But in a moment we shall see that I was able to use this knowledge by readers of the historical outcome to pace my narrative.

Dzerzhinsky Square

In the beginning of the first book, three days before the storming of the Winter Palace, my main characters are a socialist prince, a peasant, a sergeant and another peasant. They are idealists but also the hard men without whom no revolution can succeed. The fiancée of one is Anna. Within pages we meet the schoolgirl Nadezhda Alleluyeva, an idealist with a soft core, who will kill herself fifteen years later in guilt for the excesses of her husband, Joseph Stalin. She is a contrast. We meet Joseph Stalin himself, already shaped by the hard years (we will see even him change but that is not the point here). And we meet Larissa, a German socialist of sterner stuff than Nadezhda but still to be a victim. My four heroes from the beginning work first for Stalin and then for Dzerzhinsky, the founder of the Cheka. It struck the novelist Andrew Taylor, who edited the manuscript, how the cogwheels of the KGB in Soviet society were built up through my characters. Only events that shaped the characters are shown. The larger history is known: I blithely skip almost twenty years from the last Great Terror of 1937 to the year the surviving number of my heroes, now Stalin's personal executioners, together with Anna, decide to kill him. (This 'missing' history will in any event be covered more interestingly in the 'American' volume of the trilogy.) But between 1917 and 1937 I have established these men and women as having indomitably sacrificed everything for their dream. The importance of the *change* in their characters we have discussed elsewhere: it is important to the novel, but the different point we are making here simply requires that they are established as having a certain outlook appropriate to their times.

After they murder Stalin, the story again skips a decade and a half to their grandchildren in the Brezhnev era. (Again, these intervening years are not 'lost', but better told from a CIA viewpoint in another volume.) The intermediate generation is shown briefly as having seen so much upheaval that they want the peaceful life: they are technocrats, not idealists. Larissa, having survived the camps minus her fingernails, is the last idealist and considered not only odd but dangerous. The point is made, even if lightly: history changes people, not necessarily for the better. But the reader is now starting to worry that the story may be heading nowhere good.

And the reader is confirmed in this suspicion when I introduce the grandchildren as a bunch of pleasure-loving élitists, the epitome of the New Classes, aristocrats in the making. Not nobles, who earn their rights, but aristocracy which inherits them. This, too, is historically accurate, and within the story thoroughly motivated: it is what the middle generation wanted the grandchildren to become. How the last generation comes good, again under pressure of historical imperatives and the changes motivated by their environment and their own actions, is the rest of the story. But the point I hope you will take here is that they were born different from their parents.

Langley, Virginia

The 'American' volume starts with the Second World War well under way. Two generations are established. The older one consists of Americans of means who undertook public service from a sense of noblesse. The younger consists of their children and also of the new classes of rising immigrants, as well as the refugees from the tyrants of Europe. That they will react differently is obvious. That history will shape them differently, because they will each have a different mix and sum of experience of the rest of the world and therefore a different attitude to it, is a lot less obvious. I chose the historical events first and then let the events shape the characters by simply keeping firmly in mind

86

the totality of previous experience of each. Prior experience shapes expectation, and therefore reaction, differently for each of us.

In the 1950s – golden years of paranoia in America – the older generation is bewildered by the lack of goodwill on the part of the Russians. The younger generation, if in the first instance liberal, simply turn paranoid because they viewed the wartime experience differently from their parents. Those in the younger generation from the other classes, which in any event started off isolationist, and the immigrants who had been personally persecuted by the tyrants, become aggressive. All of this makes wonderful tension in the novel, of course, but note for our purposes here particularly that the third generation, the grandchildren, grow up in an atmosphere of uncertainty at home created by their parents and grandparents. Again they are born different from their parents and grandparents and in their formative years are shaped even more differently by their own contemporary history; Vietnam did not help. The rest of the story is how their personal histories and world history shape the actions and reactions of the third generation once they in turn become decision makers and shapers of history.

It's easy once you get the hang of it
Well, if you practise a lot. But in each of these books those in the separate generations have more in common with their contemporaries – across class, income, even nation and race – than with their parents or children. For the writer that is both an understanding brought about by history, and made easier to establish because readers can see it is true in the real world.

This is probably the most difficult chapter in the book to apply for yourself. First, in the chapter on character, I tell you to motivate the character from the inside out. Now I tell you he is born different from his parents, with large consequential results. Even more contrarily, I tell you that his environment and times have a very large influence and will create a different kind of character. Of course they have and will. If you don't pay your taxes, you go to jail. If you live in a police state, one night the secret police may come for you. If totalitarians take over your country, they are likely to shoot you simply because you are a writer – there is an historical pattern of such people murdering all intellectuals (the Khmer Rouge defined an intellectual as anyone with a high school education). After any of these experiences you will not be the same person. But the times will shape each character differently in his reactions. That is one way you can use history.

But now extrapolate from a person like yourself, who has probably lived in a liberal democracy all your life, and imagine a person born into a police state, growing up there without the opportunity to form your preconceptions. Would human rights to him be an axiom? Here history allows you to make large points which those who scorn it have to spend hundreds of pages establishing.

Best of all

If your characters are in a position to shape history, even in a small way, that *puts you in charge*, and you can arrange for the Good to beat the hell of the Evil.

Mining real history for your thriller

It is a commonplace that many a thriller writer mines his plots from contemporary events of the kind which will eventually feature in history books. A simpler way of looking at my Cold War series described above is as contemporary history turned into literary tension by focussing on what it did to people. We have already seen how even a casual economic historian and reader passim in the rest of history like me could mine specialist history for a novel, *The Zaharoff Commission*, which was taken seriously as real history and real economic commentary (not my intention but a flattering side dish to the ego all the same). But all this is the sort of history in which every thriller writer has at least some interest or, as an avid reader, will eventually stumble across. In the Zaharoff case I had read Donald McCormick's *Pedlar of Death: the life of Sir Basil Zaharoff* because it caught my eye on a library shelf. A tiny incident in it brought some special knowledge to bear which I had acquired while studying economic history under Tom Sheridan, merely for something to distract my mind while I wrote a violent novel and directed a couple of plays. These are the serendipities which in time become familiar to every professional thriller writer.

But what if you have a deeper interest in history or even special knowledge about a certain period of it? A professional historian read a manuscript for me and, besides historical corrections, volunteered this insightful comment: 'You think your characters lived in hard times? Try any century before the nineteenth. It is not just empty words that life was short and brutish.' That's about people! And the tension is built-in.

Add the fact that the adventure is a form of thriller that is under-served by good writers, and an interest in both history and thrillers becomes an opportunity for those with this fortunate combination of interests.

If you haven't read her yet, acquaint yourself with the books of Dorothy Dunnett. There are the Dolly books, frothy thrillers, lightweight amusements, but well written. Now turn to her Lymond saga, half a dozen thick volumes that start with *The Game of Kings*. This is romance in the grand manner, a stunning adventure. The editor writing the blurb for the Arrow paperback edition thrills to the excitement of Lymond's return from humiliating exile: 'Leading a loyal band of men who have waited for him, he now seeks to unravel the dark past over a wartorn and defeated country. For he is fighting to track down three men – one of whom holds the only answer Lymond can give to the world, parliaments and men alike who condemned him.' Sounds like a thriller, right? Perhaps one by Ted Albeury or Charles McCarry about a shamed and humiliated Germany after the Second World war? Actually, the time is 1547, and the place is Edinburgh.

Next, note the contrast to the Dolly books in literary impact. Dunnett is, of course, a fine if sometimes tart stylist in the established British manner of educated and cultured writers; one imagines that even a postcard from her would delight. But the material in Lymond turns her novels into high literature as the material in the Dollies do not. Dunnett, a professional historian, has by her choice of material elevated herself far beyond the level of the routine thriller.

If you have a deep amateur or serious interest in history, so can you.

Lest you think this is a fluke applicable only to a professional historian of Scotland, Dunnett repeated her triumph with a series of equally successful novels about an Italian merchant adventurer.

The historical adventure is a thriller form with huge built-in sales potential for those who love the source material and can handle the required scope and sweep of narrative. The extent is not limited to 100,000 words for beginners as in contemporary-subject thrillers but is expected to be in the 150–250,000 word range. That by itself offers another huge advantage: space to develop your characters.

Of course, this applies not only to general history. I imagine Bernard Cornwell's successful novels about ancient maritime manoeuvres derive from a love of maritime history, just as James Clavell's monster bestseller about the first Europeans in feudal Japan derived from an interest in the Orient.

Make a list of historical novels you have liked which are adventures or thrillers. Read them again. Now consider the history you like to read. Take a character who appeals to you and the key incident in his life. Spend some time considering the lesser characters around him and the smaller incidents which shaped him inside the large sweep of history, and suddenly you have a plot.

Nostalgia and the millennial impulse

We started this chapter on the cusp between the two great technological ages of transport and communications. We live on the cusp of two millennia.

If you have the skill, the insight and the energy to write a great millennial novel in the form of a thriller, fine. A good starter set of resources would be the Bible, the Koran and Paul Johnson's *A History of the Jews*.

Personally I would not write a millennial thriller unless I could be certain it would turn out to be *Exodus* or *Ben-Hur*, some kind of truly distinctive story with survival value. Publishers and agents are already 'glutted with the commonplace thrillers about a millennarial sect acquiring an atom bomb and auto-fulfilling their prediction of armageddon', one despairing New York editor told me when I asked him what he would like me to say about it in this book. A London editor said, 'There have been two movies called *Armageddon* already, and it's not even the new century yet. That's the kiss of death. Twice over.' A leading agent added, 'And for god's sake warn them not to stick the millennium on as a gloss. That will date their books almost instantly.' The millennium, in short, is a hat-rack breaker before it happens.

But. Our theme in this book is twofold. One: you, as a thriller reader, can write a thriller. Two: with a little thought, you can write a good thriller, perhaps even one that may survive as literature. This is a chapter aimed at those who have already gained some experience, perhaps even publication, so we do not need to stress practice and hard work, or the quality of the thought required.

Nostalgia is a subtext of many thrillers, from Ellis Peters's Brother Cadfael series to, more obviously, Harper Lee's *To Kill a Mockingbird*. Nostalgia by its often crude and trite self is a very big publishing industry, something recognized in their bones by all editors. The millennium will intensify the tendency to nostalgia. It seems quite likely that we shall have a decade or more of intense nostalgia for the twentieth century. This will be balanced by a less intense and shorter curiosity about the future, which will fade away when people grasp, as they soon must, that the mortgage and the milk bill must still be paid.

Let's deal with these impulses in reverse order.

Sci-fi thriller?

Is there scope and space for a futuristic thriller? Perhaps, if it is exceptional. But the greater likelihood is that it will fall between the two stools of genre specialization and editorial meekness. The market for hard science fiction is moribund, regardless of what technofreak editors say over their carrot juice about how much they would love to see a hard science fiction manuscript. I do not quite see how a thriller can be fitted into the conventions and readers' expectations of the dominant futurist form, the fantasy. Of course, a fantasy novel is, at least analytically, an adventure with fuzzy edges; whether it is an adventure by your definition, speaking as a thriller writer, you must decide for yourself. As far as I am concerned, Frank Herbert has already spoken the last word and from there it has been downhill. For me, fantasy is now by definition too far removed from rational cause and effect to be the concern of thriller writers.

That does, however, still leave the computer, the geometric growth in power of which is now a commonplace, cybernetics, robotics, and the interface between biology and transistors, which has become a live moral and political issue with the success of the sheep- and people-cloners. The moral and political issues of the day are the meat and drink of thriller writers. If you are interested in the technicalities or ethics of these matters, there are thriller themes for the taking but, considering the marketing problems of science fiction, it would not be clever to set your thriller too far into the future. Such themes should thus, for the aware thriller writer, not be tied to the forward-looking millennial impulse. They stand a better chance if set in the here and now; why give away the urgent tension of immediacy if you don't have to?

Look at the history of the most successful hard-science thrillers of our time. *Blade Runner*, the movie, is from an elderly Philip K. Dick story. Michael Crichton's dinosaur cloning stories, which have made him and Steven Spielberg rich, could have been written any time from Conan Doyle forward. These stories are timeless; the times just caught up with their subject matter.

Looking behind you for a thrill

The rich mine of nostalgia is an entirely less dangerous ground. Thriller writers have banked the Nazis forever, and probably will forever more. But there is much in the twentieth century which has not been mined and that offers themes and enviroments to the thriller writer looking for a period to make his own.

Ever hear of Carnaby Street? Mary Quant? Swinging London? Pinstriped Mini Coopers? The Rolling Stones? Of course, you have. They are celebrated in song and fashion.

Andrew Taylor has already started mining the gloomy period in Britain still under rationing just after the war. A couple of volumes into his planned series, it is his, he has claimed that entire Brontë-like atmosphere for himself, and anyone else is a johnny-come-lately, forced into contortions for novelty to differentiate his books from Andrew's.

But no-one has grabbed the period of light and mad release from tension and poverty which followed, which goes by the name of the Swinging Sixties: where is the Carnaby Street Detective? No-one has grabbed the suicidal Seventies in Britain when power-crazed union bosses forbade the burial of the dead. A few have used the hedonistic Eighties as background –

Campbell Armstrong created a detective with a taste for American cars and flash suits in novels like *Mambo* – but except for a couple of poor books which sank without much trace, no-one claimed the City in its Thatcherite heyday. Hell, Murray Smith, a good British writer, even looked across the Atlantic for his setting when he wanted to write a financial thriller. The sleazy Nineties have a couple of entries from failed politicians but they are a period too close to us to qualify here. But all the decades before the Second World War have much to recommend them. Stay out of the Edwardian splendour and waste: I may yet want to create a detective with a mistress who bathes in champagne!

The same applies to every other country, including one you may know better than Britain.

Not only are these periods available for the taking but, in the flow of nostalgia that follows the turn of the millennium for a decade or so, they will receive much newspaper and television publicity. The thriller writer will thus be working into a pre-existing interest in these periods.

Advanced plotting

What happens when you outgrow the simplistic forms of achieving structure which for convenience we have until now called 'plot'?

Plot as personal structure

The truth is that it doesn't matter how you structure your book. I have never liked the word 'plot', as it is too apt to take on in the mind of novices, and a few careless teachers too, an identity and importance of its own separated from the characters, which is a nonsense. When you find yourself 101% in agreement with this sentiment, you are ready to move on.

For alternative methods, look for organizing or hierarchical forms in your own life that you are comfortable with.

Thirty years ago, just out of university, I was a trainee in an advertising agency. In those more spacious days a creative team consisted of a writer, a visualizer and a graphic artist. The writer had ideas and provided text. The visualizer imagined how the disparate pieces of text and illustration would look on the page.

The graphic artist performed the technical functions of laying down typography and pasting down photographs. My training in various departments put me in contact with such teams. I never actually worked permanently in one, because when my training was completed I was pulled into management as a floating troubleshooter. But occasionally, in a crisis, I would work for a day or two with such a team. Those were some of the happiest days of my life.

A few years ago I mentioned this recollection at a conference, in response to a question about my background. Afterwards the late Frank Muir told me he recognized the method. He and Dennis Norden (one of the most famous of all comedy teams) had worked the same way in their glory years, with the director and producer fulfilling the functions of visualizer and technical assistance. Those, he said, were the happiest days of his life.

Clearly, the details are not the same. My own experience writing a weekly comedy half-hour was terrifying. I used to dictate the script in my car on the way to work. It won some prizes and was wondrously well paid. But the experience was so stressful that I have never again undertaken comedy except in collaboration or as one-liners. Muir, by contrast, breathed comedy as I breathe thrills.

However, the writing of advertising and comedy are both very much akin to writing a thriller. Advertising must grab immediately or it is a dead loss. Comedy must be properly arranged so as to put the punchline last and prepare the audience for it. Both fail if they lose tension. These are matters of structure that clearly slide over into the instant presentation of characters people want to identify with or know more about. At this level of condensation 'plot' is, therefore, simply subsumed into character.

Though I never discussed it with him, it would not be difficult to imagine that even the urbane Muir might fret under the disciplines and rigidities of advertising work, in which I flourished.

I still see a thriller organizationally as the large idea the writer has, followed by the sketch where the visualizer arranges the components so that they make maximum sense together, followed by the hard technical graft of laying down the letters and words and pictures in the right order and relation to each other, to make a whole larger than the sum of the parts.

The key point at which this now obsolete advertising method locks with my view of the thriller is at the visualizer. Advertising is a disjunctive form. One tells only what is essential to understanding, and fills in the gaps with pictures and clever conjunctions of arrangement and typeface selection. The thriller, as I practice it anyway, is also a disjunctive form. I tell the reader only what is essential and fill in the holes with the pictures the arrangement of my crucial bits create in his mind.

It suits me, it suits my readers, it suits reviewers who can say that the novel is 'visual', it suits film people who can 'see' the story but yet know that it leaves plenty of irrelevant (to me) surrounding detail for them to be 'creative' with.

Len Deighton is a thriller writer with a minimalist style but very intricate and subtle plots, in one fabulous instance carried for nine volumes in the three trilogies about Bernard Samson. I would not be surprised to discover that he has carried forward, consciously or subconsciously, a similar outlook to mine, from his own days in advertising in New York.

I'm not suggesting my version of advertising agency creative groupings to you as a particular method. For the unskilled it is dangerously littered with potholes. Thirty years ago I could probably not have used it for novel-length work either. But for the practised writer of my peculiar background it fits like an old glove. It helps me simplify, whereas for someone else it might simply leave too many loose questions lurching across the deck like loaded cannon.

What I am suggesting is that when you grow out of the simplistic methods we must all start with – which served me so well when I started that I wrote this book to share them – and want to see if a more advanced structuring paradigm will not improve the quality of your writing, you should consider your day job and life to see what else you are comfortable with in the present or remember fondly from the past in the way of hierarchical structures or working methods or other sequential behaviour patterns. You're looking for something you are quietly happy with, so it may be as unobtrusive as to be almost invisible. Look hard at obvious things that you would normally overlook precisely because they already fit you like an old glove.

If you are a lawyer, an accountant, a doctor or one of a dozen other types of professional, you already have professional structures. If you are a churchgoer, you hear structures every Sunday. If you are a lay officer of your church, you have more structures available, but do look to the structures above the lay officers that you take so much for granted. Your favourite sport or game has structures both on and off the court, in its performance, in its public presentation, in its organization, regulation and management. These are all structures you know but are subsuming unexamined precisely because they are so familiar. There may be profit in examining the familiar consciously.

A *freebie from the familiar*

Chances are that sometime today you will either watch television or at least pick up the television guide to discover why you shouldn't bother to switch on the idiot box. Television fiction and documentaries, if they are any good, are all structure, though the structures are varied and often imaginative. The television guide is itself a very professionally structured document.

Please don't think this last about television is a trivial suggestion. One afternoon recently I decided to start the same evening on a novel about motor racing. I was once a motor racer, so I would do my minimal amount of 'colour' research (about racetracks which were built after I retired) when I finished the first draft, concentrating instead on the characters. But I needed a structure. After dinner my family watched a film on video. As the cassette was being inserted. I caught a glimpse on television of a grand prix being broadcast and asked if we could watch that instead of the film. (The film, which we watched after the race, had a dully predictable structure.)

Right after the grand prix finished, I had my structure: the book would be structured like a race. Obvious, eh? Perhaps. I *had* spent two hours thinking about it while riding my bicycle in the lanes and not thought of the solution until I saw the race. It had an established, yet somehow odd, rhythm, split between the race and the commentators, which I thought would be exciting in a thriller, building the tension in unexpected ways. There was a certain distance, covered by edgy smiles, between the overly familiar commentators and the drivers coolly risking their lives for untold wealth, and I was struck by the mistakes about drivers and their attitudes the commentators made while telling not a single lie. This gave me an idea for a viewpoint of great subtlety, woven into a grid of duplicity that in the writing of the novel threw off sparkling interplays between the characters. With structure and presentation (viewpoint as hidden counterpoint) decided, in essence a whole novel 'visualized', I was able to start the book on page 1 and write it to the end without ever writing down any 'plot'. The structure itself threw up events which illuminated my characters. I expect that readers will be both excited and comforted by the correspondence between familiar television viewing and the flow of my novel.

Not all television is a waste of time!

What have we learned in a chapter devoted to the more advanced writer, one with a lot of hard practice and possibly even publication already behind him, definitely more confident that he is *thinking* like a thriller writer? Not the specifics – they are only examples – but the generality, the tone?

It is possible to break the rules, to reach into yourself for something you probably always had but have never fully realized, and to use it to elevate your novels above mere publishability. What you elevate them to – we have used literary merit, long-term survival as books readers want to read and subtlety in presentation as desiderata in the examples – is up to you.

7. Sustenance from the stacks: research

The wise author does as little formal research as possible without skimping the job. If that sounds contradictory from a writer whose dustjackets invariably carry extracts from reviews praising his thorough research, it is not because I am two-faced. The plain fact is that research is extremely time-consuming – time perhaps better spent writing. Oh, I loved research when I started out and so did most other authors I know – many still do, but the critical enquirer need not scratch deep to discover that almost all of us have at one time or another extended research unnecessarily merely to postpone that terrifying moment when we have to sit down at the computer and *actually start writing*.

Unfortunately it is not possible to help you by laying down a hard and fast rule: so much research for so many pages of double-spaced text – such stupidity would strain even academic credulity. The best I can do is to help you minimize the time spent on research by suggesting when, what and how to research, and how to make the maximum use of the facts discovered from the minimum of time spent in formal research.

Informal research

As suggested when we discussed the sources of your concepts and characters (Chapter 3), you are continuously engaged in research whenever you read a newspaper or a book whether fiction or non-fiction, whenever you listen to the radio or watch television, whenever you are abroad and observing people. Images and facts and novel connections between them are retained in your mind and become part of your subconscious knowledge, often without your being consciously aware of the process – this is what psychologists mean when they use the jargon word 'subliminal'.

Little conscious effort is required to guide your leisure non-fiction reading into paths productive to your writing; for the committed writer this will happen naturally. After all, if you write the kind of fiction you like reading, you probably also like reading the same type of non-fiction as other authors in the same field. As a result, you may already know a great deal of use to a thriller writer that someone else who reads, say, only romances, will have to learn afresh. Because your leisure activities are in tune with your professional aspirations, you should therefore not need to do huge amounts of general research merely for background purposes. As a bonus, you will never have to search for the concept of your next book because your chosen mental environment will suggest more themes than you can ever use.

The right frame of mind minimizes the time you need to take from your writing and give to research.

What not to research

If you have no emotional commitment for or against something, all the research in the world won't make you convincing to readers. This does not apply only to characters (missionaries in my case) you as a person find dull, but in all things great and small. For instance, I have no feeling for firearms and have only once owned one because crocodiles were trying to eat me and people were shooting at me. I would therefore never include a gun nut in any of my books. Characters in my novels, regardless of their skill with firearms, regard firearms either as necessary evils or tools of their trade. I choose this example because guns would be easy to research if I didn't already know something about them. It is not command of the facts that is important but emotional commitment. Because I cannot understand other people's emotional commitment to firearms, any time I write about a gun nut, he gets sent up – which is fine as long as you are writing comedy but there are many characters who need guns that I don't want to send up. So, I give people with guns characteristics I can comprehend and sympathize with or at least pity. Paradoxically, if I were violently anti-firearms, I would also be able to write about a gun nut in such a way that readers could share my antipathy. If you find characters you have written are dull or caricatured, check that you haven't substituted research for the emotional commitment that comes with either empathy or antipathy.

The fiction writer should never have to do primary research, i.e. research from the original materials rather than other people's non-fiction books. Original research is painfully time-consuming and often unproductive. The only exception to this rule is the use of diaries and letters to discover the speech cadences and vocabulary of another time or place – and even here you might learn more, and more quickly, from other fiction writers, including playwrights, who have covered the same ground before. Until you try it, you will not believe the amount of time primary research can consume. I spent four years on Zaharoff without uncovering a single significant fact not already in Donald McCormick's biography. All I had to show for my pains were the extracts from diaries and other reports of what my real characters had actually said, which I used (sometimes out of the original context) as dialogue wherever I could – and which gave the whole book an uneven tone and persuaded ignorant critics that my dialogue was 'anachronistic'!

A handy balance between what and not?

There is a vast swathe of tiny bits of necessary knowledge that can suck you into its details and waste your time. In recent years I have shortcut a huge amount of time-consuming work in the library and on the phone by keeping the Oxford Reference Shelf on CD-ROM permanently in the CD-ROM drive of my Mac; it is also available for the Windows computers. It contains in a very handy format dictionaries of abbreviations (acronyms), business, computing, law, science, English, translation dictionaries for French, German, Italian and Spanish, a gazetteer (worth the price by itself!), and writer's and editor's dictionaries of English and science and usage, plus a collection of quotes that won't replace Bartlett for serious literary work but which is more than adequate for a thriller writer. I work on the assumption that anything so esoteric that I cannot look up in the Oxford Reference Shelf, and which is not utterly essential to the main character of my novel in the conduct of his affairs, will also be irrelevant to my readers. That limits research to the finer details of the work and environment of my main characters, as described in the rest of this chapter.

Sit down firmly before reading

This is an example of the horrifying waste of time that tiny bits of necessary information can cost. It arose in my most recent novel. It is not an isolated example.

A character, whom the reader will shortly discover has literary aspirations, lists the functions of the troubleshooter to a motor racing équipe as chekist, vindicatore* and, – hmm, a Hebrew word the meaning of which I know without being able to recall the word. Far too esoteric for my trusty Oxford. I think the word might be *bulvon*, but am vaguely dissatisfied with it. I leave it aside and make a note to investigate later. After I finish the novel, I check on the Internet: the phonetic Hebrew dictionary that used to be there is gone and I can't use Hebrew script on my computer and, anyway, how do you look up a word you don't know in a script you can't write – a Kafkaesque notion. I call the rector of my local parish. He is not a Hebrew scholar but will enquire. I call a bishop I know. Too esoteric for him but he will consult a reference at the university for me in a week or so when he lectures there. There is no synagogue listed in the telephone directory for any of the cities in Ireland, where I live. I call an Israeli politician who taught me economics in the States; he speaks only modern Hebrew and isn't speaking to any rabbi because the rabbis are all in his opposition. I call Jewish friends around the world and set enquiries in train. Finally the rector calls back and says he can't help but he knows the name of the head of the tiny Jewish community in the nearby city, who is a retired lawyer and a scholar. At this point it has taken several days and a great deal of money to check a single word, and I am still stuck with my first guess, which now really nags me. The elderly lawyer immediately tells me my first guess, *bulvon*, is Yiddish for an obstreperous person, a violent buffoon, altogether wrong for what I want. But he doesn't know the Hebrew word for the meaning I want either, though he believes the concept is a technical one in Mosaic law; he is too ill to undertake research, though if I want to wait a couple of months

---

*The first Bolshevik secret police were called the Cheka and its members chekisti. The vindicatore is an assassin who avenges insults to the touchy pride or purse of a Sicilian family; the most famous Mafia avenger in literature is Richard Condon's manic creation of Charley Partanna, vindicatore to the Prizzis, memorably played on screen by Jack Nicholson.

until he finishes a course of treatment... He arranges for me to call someone else. Another half a day slides by before I track this fellow down at his golf club. He thinks he knows but can't be certain and so gives me a number for the Chief Rabbi of Ireland. By now it is sundown on Friday and it would be stupid to telephone a Jew on his Sabbath. Two more days slide by until office hours on Monday. At last I ask the secretary to ask the Chief Rabbi the Hebrew word which means 'a friend of the family who in a blood feud may act as if he were a member of the family' and she returns in seconds with the correct name: 'goel hadam'. One week of work to discover a single phrase.

I wrote the entire first draft of that 130,000 word novel in eighteen days. Life is not fair, and in a writer's life research is the unkindest cut of all.

But the book turns on the meaning of that word, even though it is used only twice, once in setting up the plot and once as a valedictory at the end of the story. I could fudge it but it wouldn't be the same. And if I get it wrong and even one critic discovers that I got it wrong – it doesn't bear thinking about. It is necessary work.

If you wish to be a professional writer you should view this chapter as a guide to reducing such necessary but time-consuming work to an absolute minimum.

When to research

You should do as much of your research as possible *after* you have finished your first draft. This has the signal advantage that you will then be searching for specific facts, rather than reading at random in the vague hope of recognizing something useful.

Imagine three books: in the first, the main character is an old car nut ('a vintage automobile enthusiast') and the plot concerns crooked dealings in pre-War motors; in the second, the same old car nut is framed for murder by a baddie who doesn't know a Duesenberg from a Delage from a Delahaye; in the third, a character requires a fast and luxurious car. Now, if you know nothing about old cars and have no interest in them, it is not likely you will write a story turning on such cars, but let us say, hypothetically, that you are attempting such an awkward thing.

To write the first book you will obviously have to read many references to discover the 'feel' of the subject and talk to real old car enthusiasts before you can create the characters or write the book. You can then choose a suitable make of car and concentrate on the details of that. Afterwards you will have to double-check all the facts you wrote into your novel.

In the second book, where the character is into old cars but the plot does not hinge on that fact, a general, coffee-table book about old cars will be enough introduction, plus a single standard work on the particular old car your hero drives, plus a chapter from a book explaining the skills required to operate hand-throttles, ignition advance, rear wheel-only brakes, crash gearbox and so forth. If you didn't somehow discover that these things are important, you could look foolish, which is why I prefer writing about things I already have some grounding in and commitment to. Afterwards you would have to check all your facts.

In the third instance, where you merely want a fast, luxurious car, you can leave a blank space in the writing (as I did in the section above) and check the 629 Dewey category of books or magazines the next time you're at the library – or ask someone in the pub. At this point you might learn something more about the chosen car than that it is fast and luxurious, and include a telling detail or two in the action of your next draft.

To summarize, you should put off research as long as you can, preferably until you have your first draft in hand and know exactly which specific facts you wish to discover or check. Once you start writing, this advice is not as astounding as it sounds because you will find that your attention is where it should be, on the characters and their development, rather than on mere dry facts which you may or may not be able to work into the action; the action then dictates the research and that's how it should be.

What to research, where and how

The bane of the modern thriller is educated readers. Even small errors will forfeit the confidence of your reader, so it is essential to present every fact absolutely spot-on. It helps that librarians are keen to help bona fide authors and will borrow from other libraries virtually any book or periodical you care to name.

At the most basic level, you must spell brand names right and pitch them at the right socio-economic level and in the correct chronology. In 1960, a psychiatrist would have told one proudly, without prompting, 'That's my red Jag over there,' but a generation later his car would rank lower on his list of status symbols than attendance at international symposia and would probably be a Mercedes rather than a Jaguar. You discover this by calling his professional body and asking them which possession or activity their members prize most highly; if they refuse to tell you, talk to student psychiatrists about their aspirations, which are likely to mirror closely those of the peer group to which they aspire. And check who advertises in professional magazines or in publications targeted to your character's peer group. One distinctly upper-class writer of lower-class characters reads three wretched tabloids every day 'as an alternative to going out and actually meeting that sort of people'.

Next, you must check the operational details of any machines that you show in action. Thriller readers all seem to be machine freaks. Don't make the mistake of believing something is too esoteric to matter. Andrew McCoy, to cut a few words of repetitive description in *Atrocity Week*, called a control in a helicopter 'a throttle' rather than 'a collective pitch control and throttle lever' and, he says, 'Now I can't go into a bar without running into some helicopter pilot who thinks I'm an ignoramus. There are only a few thousand helicopter pilots in all the world and they've all read my book.' I had a similar experience with *Reverse Negative*: I'm not ignorant about computers (I'm the author of a standard computer text and the general editor of a series on computer graphics) but I shortcut some technicalities on the assumption that most readers wouldn't know and that those who did couldn't care less. They could and did: at least a dozen have mentioned it to me.

One way of building reader confidence in you, the author, is to particularize *everything*. Don't put your man on a plane to Paris, put him on a specific flight or at least on a specified airline. Ask a travel agent to let you have old copies of their Blue and Red Books so that you can look up the flight number or at least check that the airline flies to Paris. Products, places, things, arrangements can all be particularized.

Besides your library, professional bodies, a friendly travel agent and the body of opinion to be found in any bar, it is useful to have a contact at a newspaper of record or one of the news magazines. Such a friend can look up the reference you seek on his terminal via the index of the newspaper's archive, all in a few minutes, while you might spend days at your library scrolling microfilm and perhaps never find the reference. Social contacts with a doctor, a lawyer and other professionals are also desirable because it is astounding how often technical, professional points arise. University teachers, if approached right, will usually do a brief translation over the phone and spell out the words for you. I obtain my Biblical quotes from the vicar and call a bishop on matters of high theology and for information on Islam; a Jesuit I met while having my appendix out gave me a far more useful comprehension of the Irish sense of injustice than two IRA men I sought out at personal risk; the local priest tells me anything I want to know about the Catholic mind and outlook. If you intend to use your friends and friends' friends like this, it helps to show willing to give some time in return: for instance, recently I spent two hours on the phone with a journalist, a friend of my publisher's personal assistant, explaining about South Africa.

The Internet

The promise of instant information on request has so far for most of us been disappointing, not because there is too little of it, but because there is such a huge flow of low-grade information that it is difficult and time-consuming to pick out the nuggets of gold. I live five minutes on foot from my library and find that often it is quicker to go there and discover what I want to know than to look it up on the Internet.

Nonetheless, you should keep in mind that the Internet does not only comprise the worldwide web, the news groups and e-mail. There are other significant facilities in which you might find the learning-time repaid. Two that I like are Telnet and FTP. Telnet has a poor interface but is in use at many reference libraries. I use it to discover before I travel twenty miles whether the various college libraries closest to me have the books I want to refer to. It also impresses librarians if you can tell them in which library the book you want them to request 'on the Inter-library' is kept. My own county and city lending libraries will buy any books or stack of books I ask for, but it repays their investment with a little courtesy to give them all the required information including ISBN numbers, publishers, even book-sellers or wholesalers who have the books in stock. The Internet shines when required to do no more than deliver cataloguing information.

FTP (file transfer protocol) has several good interfaces for most computers. It is useful for downloading entire documents. Often documents of a much higher standard than are available on the worldwide web are available only by FTP.

The world wide web or WWW is useful for an overview, and sometimes to discover where useful documents are held. It also brings news as fast as the television and the newspaper do.

However, I have found that by far the most useful research instrument on the web is the news group. There is a news group for every conceivable interest on something called the Usenet, seamlessly accessible through your browser under 'news' or 'discussions' or agreeable interfaces usually available free of charge or for low cost. In every news group you will find world-class experts and idiots. It takes a little time to sort the wheat from the chaff, but that is easily done by asking a simple question to which you already know the answer. From there you proceed to discuss by private e-mail the more difficult matters with the experts who have revealed themselves.

It may be smart to start a thread on any news group or mailing list where you are a regular for the surfers to describe briefly what they do besides the common interest which binds the news group together. You never know whose skills and interests you may require for your next book! In that sense, news groups and mailing lists are like gentlemen's clubs writ large.

There are also mailing lists on which a higher level still of expertise is available. Some are moderated and semi-private and some are restricted by invitation to professionals.

My example is fortuitous but none the less powerful for all that.

I met Peter Allen, who is a pharmacist in Melbourne on the other side of the world, in a mailing list dedicated to audiophiles. A couple of years later I offered him my latest manuscript to read because a book of mine he wanted was out of print. Part of the story concerns cocaine that a trouble-shooter confiscated and washed down the lavatory but must now hand back to the owners because they hold his girl hostage for it. In my first draft the character substituted plaster of Paris plus just a little cocaine bought on the street. Peter did not like the plaster of Paris at all, writing to me: 'Cocaine, if pure, is light, flaky, sparkly even, and moves in loose clumps. Legitimately cocaine is used in a spray to deaden the nasal passages when an ENT specialist goes down with a spoon and fork and a miner's lamp, several inches into someone's head to look around... I've sent this message to my pharmacy list: "Since it's New Year, perhaps our Moderator will indulge a frivolous piece of research for a friend who's writing a thriller and is 'as pure as the driven snow': What would you use as a look-alike for Cocaine Hydrochloride powder? Surely not plaster of Paris."' Out of this I got several facts I had not known before. Of course the friendship I struck up via the Internet with Peter is serendipitous, but so are most of any writer's friendships which are eventually professionally useful. But without knowing him I would not have been aware of his pharmacy mailing list.

Such examples lead me to conclude that for most writers the Internet will be a boon not so much for the information openly available as for the power of its networking (in the human rather than the technical sense) and the resultant instant and costless access to privately and professionally held specialist information.

Specialist research – do you really need it?

Specialist research is more than just the rare or esoteric books the bigger libraries keep in the stacks and bring out on request. It is research in specialist sources or by specialist researchers into rare and wonderful subjects, though you should realize that what for me may be rare and wonderful, for you might be commonplace. For instance, I need an interpreter to find my way around an index of medical extracts whereas a hypochondriac friend with absolutely no formal biological or chemical training reads it as if it were written in English. Check the location of university and technical college libraries. They contain a lot of this sort of stuff and are also a marketplace where you can meet cheap labour (students) to decipher the sanskrit for you.

There are computer databases you can refer to either via your own computer and the telephone, or by writing to them and receiving half-a-ton of print-out in return. They tend to specialize in medicine or accounting or science or defence and so on but I have yet to find one which offers much that patient work in a good university library won't uncover. They are very expensive. They do not offer the interpretative insight of personal contact with the relevant professional, as in the pharmacological example above.

You can also hire professional researchers, who are listed in author's reference books like *Writers' & Artists' Yearbook*, but you should choose one who specializes in whatever it is you want to find out (not easy for really specialized subjects) and do agree a price beforehand. If you can't be bothered with research or if your time for writing is already limited but your purse is not, this may be an option.

You may have no choice except to use professional researchers but I would make any sacrifice to do my own. One very professional writer, who has a great deal of experience in using outside researchers, wrote a novel set in the Regency period, with research provided by a hired hand. After his book was published, I discovered to my astonishment that he had never heard of Captain Gronow, the most famous and perceptive social diarist of the period. His researcher must have been either slack or stupid. But the writer had no way of finding out about Gronow because he saw only the researcher's digests, in which the good captain made no appearance. If the writer had read the raw material himself, multiple references to the key source would surely have led him to the main man's diaries and, I am absolutely certain, to creating an even better novel.

Too little research and too much

Too little research is most obvious when a writer has his facts wrong. But there is another sense in which too little research can be harmful to a novel, easily spotted by the novel making a 'thin' impression, reading like comic-book blurbs without the pictures. When not a result of faulty characterization (a common cause dealt with in Chapters 4, 8 and 9), this is often the out-come of indolence rather than lack of skill. When a writer sets a novel in New York without ever having been there, the reader need never find out, as long as the writer has done his home-work at the travel shelves of his library or on the Internet, which is good on travel-related information. It is the writer who has never been to New York and who hasn't done his homework who offends our sense of what is fit. Paradoxically, it is easier to get away with this kind of slackness about esoteric places, say the upper reaches of the Amazon – until your laziness catches up with you next year when the Amazon comes into the news or several documentaries about it are all screened at once and everybody knows all the facts.

Too much research is bad if it shows in your finished text. You must not let your newly-acquired expertise lead you into exhibitionism. I have been slammed by critics for technical exhibitionism and in each case it was the result of some editor, who had heard me expound technical detail over lunch, whining when I finished the novel that I hadn't put in all the 'hot stuff' and insisting that I do so. (With commissioned novels, where the author is paid up front, it is difficult to refuse because one would then lay oneself open to accusations of breach of faith by not delivering exactly what one had seemed to promise. How-ever, though all of my own novels were and are commissioned, the commissioned novel is a rarity.) These days, with a bit more faith in my judgement, I resist much more strenuously sugges-tions that I cast restraint to the winds. But your problem is that you haven't my intervening experience and consequent greater faith in your judgement, and you need a rule of thumb to help you judge how much is enough.

Foundations

First, of background expertise you can never have too much, as long as it is subsumed into the action rather than flung at the reader in indigestible static chunks. Nobody slammed *The Zaharoff Commission* for technical exhibitionism, perhaps because most critics aren't economists. Yet it is on one level, as an historian reviewing it for a serious journal commented, an intense study of the politico-economic mechanisms active in the defeat and collapse of what was then the most modern economy in the world; another scholarly reviewer called it a portrait of an established élite order committing suicide, which is pretty much the same thing seen from a sociological viewpoint. It is clear the level of expertise required by the economics and historical reconstruction in *Zaharoff* is far higher than that required by the more mechanical machinations in *Sinkhole*. In addition, there is physically *more* of this expertise displayed in *Zaharoff* (in that the economic condition and political will of Germany are the central theme of the novel) than in *Sinkhole*, yet it passed unmentioned in *Zaharoff* except by like-minded specialists, and was damned in *Sinkhole* by a notable few. The distinction is therefore not of expert content, but the more snobbish one between non-mechanical and mechanical technical content: expertise with explosives and grappling irons is exhibitionist, expertise at political economy is laudable! There is not a great deal you can do about it, except to exercise far greater restraint with mechanical expertise than non-mechanical and try even harder to integrate the mechanical expertise unobtrusively into your story.

The five per cent solution

My second rule of thumb is that research must behave like an iceberg, only even more discreetly! An iceberg shows one-tenth above water – but I aim for only one-twentieth of my knowledge on some subject to show, leaving the rest to illuminate the novel subtly. Recognizing the five per cent that will show is easy if you observe two selection criteria: only those facts which are most easily and most relevantly introduced into *essential action* should be included. Where there is conflict or choice, select the fact or example the least number of your readers (including specialists in the field) are likely to know.

The writer's authority

There is a general sense of authority created by some authors who foster the impression that they know what they are talking about and that you can trust them to have done their homework. Frederic Forsyth is a master of this. It is done by selecting from your five per cent of selected research those items which, while relevant to the essential action, have the striking additional quality that they impart to the reader the impression that you have done *more* than your homework, that you are an expert. If these items can then be thoroughly integrated into the action of your main set pieces, at which your reader's perception is in any event heightened by tension, the job is done. Restraint is the watchword here: don't hold up the action to show off information.

The single telling detail
Sometimes, reading the first few pages of a novel, you find yourself prepared to give yourself over totally to the writer. This is, of course, the result of many things but, if you analyze such novels carefully, you will almost always find a phrase or sentence that establishes the writer's supreme authority beyond doubt.

Experienced writers search very hard for that single telling detail, not only to impress their research, but to bring characters and places alive. In *Zaharoff*, I had the premiers of England and France visit Basil Zaharoff in the middle of a war and, in their presence, seated at his table for thirty-six with its solid gold settings, had him make up the green salad – and then topped it all by having this pedlar of death confess that, if he had not been a steelmaster, he would have loved to be a master chef. (All of this actually happened but not simultaneously.) Since readers already knew I was dealing with real people in a thoroughly researched historical context, this almost absurd detail was not ludicrous, as it would have been elsewhere, but mentioned by three of my editors as the touch that convinced them I was really 'inside' Zaharoff. If I knew such bizarre secrets, who could possibly doubt my authority subsequently (where I would tread at times on very shaky ground)?

The fudge
If you don't know something, you should find out. If you cannot find out – and the only thing I ever failed to *confirm* was the colour of J. Edgar Hoover's BVDs (underpants) for my novel *Eight Days* in Washington – you should either write your tale so the information becomes unnecessary or fudge it.

Let's say you have never been to Australia but your character is walking down a street in an expensive Australian suburb.

Expensive suburbs have trees but the only Australian tree-name you know is Eucalyptus and you want something more. If you are not naming the suburb, you can fudge by saying, 'Weird that such a posh suburb has no trees, not even a eucalyptus.' Obviously, you cannot name a real suburb unless you *know* whether it has trees. If you are naming the suburb and you know it is a safe bet there will be at least eucalypti, you can have one character answer a question by a stranger, 'Everybody knows eucalyptus wood makes a good barbie and who cares about the rest?' (If you don't know 'barbie' is Australian for barbeque, your character shouldn't be wandering around there.) In *Festival* I solved the question in more specific form – besides eucalypti, what are the trees in front of Elder Conservatoire in Adelaide? – by making the character, a Polish musician, think pointedly, mistakenly that they were all eucalypti, thereby under-lining his otherness.

Exotic settings

Unfortunately for the untravelled, thriller writers are more and more expected to provide exotic settings as what was previously exotic becomes the haunt of the cheap package tour. Fortunately, lovingly detailed descriptions are no longer de rigueur.

If you want to know about the upper Amazon, your friendly local travel agent can supply a glossy brochure. You can read Victorian explorers' accounts which are good for those single telling details as well as general ambience and far more detailed observation than modern travel writers, who all seem to fancy themselves littérateurs. You might be able to talk to people who have been there. You might even be able to go there on your holiday. (However, I have been there and the visit quite destroyed the romance of the idea of the upper Amazon for me.)

As a matter of principle, I do not write about places I have not been, but it may be that I could write more interestingly about places whose romance remains intact through unfamiliarity. You may find it persuasive that several novelists who do weird and wonderful settings very convincingly refuse to travel but have shelves groaning under Fodor and Baedeker. I mentioned the Internet to one of these and he swore. 'All those pictures! Turning the world into a village. Demystifying everything!'

Boon or bust?

He surely believes in the novel as the last frontier of romance. I merely took his words as a warning that, as a thriller writer who could lose a whole book on a single glaringly wrong fact, I should take extra care with my locations – and all other veri-fiable facts – in the global village of the communications age.

That, I am sorry to have to tell you, will be the major impact of the communications age on the thriller writer. Not that the Internet makes research easier for him, but that it gives the instant power to check his every fact to his meanest critic.

The stakes have been raised out of all proportion to the gain. Suspension of disbelief, a useful literary concept of several cen-turies' standing, has suddenly for thriller writers become an accusation rather than a versatile tool and expectation. Technical details which once had a shelf life measured in decades now become boring commonplaces in less time than it takes to write, sell and publish a novel.

How you respond is up to you. Many will simply quadruple-check, and a large number will overload their thrillers with all the 'hard stuff' the information explosion offers. I think the more fool they. For myself, I shall fall back on what has always served me best, characters readers want to know, and leave the hard technicalities and instantly over-exposed locations to those who do not mind if their books have a shelf life of weeks.

Research, then, is a means of providing a realistic backdrop for the actions of characters. At a minimum, there must be no tears in the backdrop and no visible blotches of paint as in outright errors or obvious fudges. At a maximum, in the best thrillers, research can provide an aura of authority to the writer who uses it with discretion and restraint, and the discipline never to let its 'product' infringe on the space his characters must develop in.

113

8. Writer's Blues: breaching the blocks

Laymen speak of 'a writer's block' as if it were singular and are often encouraged in this fallacy by authors who are understandably reluctant to discuss something as personal as mental impotence. There are many kinds of writers' blocks and probably as many reasons for blocks as there are reasons for writing, but they do fall into three conveniently discussed categories:

- blocks in the development of your fictional characters;
- blocks in the forward motion of the plot;
- blocks personal to you-the-writer, evidenced as an inability to write.

You want the write frame of mind

We shall investigate the causes and effects of – and remedies for – a number of blocks under each heading, but it may be possible for you to avoid ever facing most of these blocks if you recognize that most of them are the result of an unprofessional attitude to your vocation and that those few blocks inherent in the profession (i.e. liable to attack hardened professionals as well as novices) can be ameliorated by the right attitude.

The right attitude is this: **a writer writes**.

If you merely want the ego-boost of calling yourself an author or a novelist, fine, you can afford to strike poses of almost unbearable suffering for your 'art' and you should study this chapter avidly as instruction in sado-masochistic imagination-expansion.

If you want to be a professional, published novelist, you will do your best to beat the blocks by never allowing them to happen to you. And it is here that the right attitude, your utter commitment to writing *as an activity*, is so important because the writer who regularly *writes* improves skills which, when lacking, create blocks. He also builds, through disciplined experience at his keyboard, the confidence to overcome those blocks inherent to the profession.

Unblocking characters

When blocked characters almost never happen to you, you can consider yourself a time-served craftsman because your skill at characterization will by definition be highly developed.

Underdeveloped characterization skills

The corollary of this is that most character blocks that trouble the prentice writer result from underdeveloped skill or carelessness or simple laziness. In most cases reference to Chapter 4 should provide a solution. Two examples will suffice.

A common complaint in writers' circles and from teachers in writing schools concerns the character who grows so monstrously that he crowds out the other characters. This Falstaff syndrome is a variation of a character running away with the author and the simple remedy is ruthless cutting and pruning. Put the bastard on a diet and if that doesn't solve the problem, have another character kill him or do it yourself by writing him out. This suggestion is likely to be met with howls of outrage – I objected when it was first made to me – but a brutal assessment of the character's real value to the action, as opposed to the 'literary impact' of the fine writing which has created him, will soon expose him as a mere indulgence of the author and therefore unaffordable to the would-be professional.

This sort of character is also very often the one that prevents the pseuds and poseurs from being published because they can't bear to kill so much fine description – especially as it is often autobiographical. William Faulkner told us to murder our darlings!

Or take the character at a dead-end, who has developed so very far in a direction from which he can no longer be brought back into the mainstream of the plot that he threatens to ruin the whole novel. This is merely another authorial indulgence and the remedies are the same, with the exception that a really hard look at your draft might reveal the point where he went wrong and you could then save all the pages before. However, my personal experience is that it is easier in the long run to start at the beginning with a new or at least renamed character in the part.

We've already agreed that you must have an emotional charge about each character, either pro or con. But this implies only that you should approve or disapprove of each character, rather than being neutral. Loving your characters impartially like a stern father meting out just and proportionately fair punishment to the wicked and rewards to the good is desirable, being *in love* with any single character leads to disaster.

These apparent blocks are therefore not true blocks but part of your learning process.

True character blocks

The character blocks the professional runs into very often follow logically from the actions of his characters bringing the plot to an unforeseen point. For instance, there arises an unavoidable requirement for a minor character of a sort you consider dull, let's say a missionary when you already know you don't do good missionaries. Or an important character for whom you had high hopes turns out a dud and can absolutely not be written out. How can you surmount a lack of emotional commitment to a character or revive a dud in the second draft? The tricks of the trade are the same:

Stereotype reversal
Take the aforesaid missionary to whom you have no emotional commitment and therefore always do badly when you write him straight or, worse, as an unintentional send-up. But what if, instead of presenting him as a doddering do-gooder and would-be holy man, you made him a thorough bad penny who chose the mission fields because he likes fornicating with black women, who is a cruel, miserable old cuss, who's too slovenly to conduct prayers properly, and who so lacks perception that he has not noticed the excellent voices in the choir? Perhaps you could do such a character better; it is less likely that an evil character will be mistaken for a caricature than an incredibly good one.

Character grafts

Take a surplus character and merely graft his characteristics onto the character you have difficulty creating. Obviously, the donor character must have his own credibility and interest. This process creates the most interestingly tortured Dostoievskian characters, torn between opposites. But be careful you don't let a minor character hog all the reader's interest.

The same process can be used if, for space and pace, you cut characters. The characteristics of the superfluous characters are grafted onto the remaining characters and the action in the next draft is rewritten to make allowance, with the result that virtually always the novel is enriched by the conflict within as well as between characters.

With this in mind, whenever I have to cut a finished novel, I remain alert for brief flashes from the cut sections that might be inserted in the remainder as enriching contrasts.

Role reversal

A variation, often used in romances, is the brief role reversal. For instance, the hunter becomes the hunted and so reveals new facets of both characters. This instantly suggests new action/plot possibilities too. Shakespeare's *Much Ado About Nothing* uses role reversal in the most blatant form possible and it is a standard method in comedies of a certain age.

As an aside, the advanced writer can use role reversal positively as a character-building method, as long as it is done subtly. In my just-finished novel, the narrator tells his story in the first person. He is secretive and duplicitous, and he knows it. The reader wonders why he admits to so much. At the end of the novel we discover he did not really tell his own story, that it was told for him by his girl, who at the beginning of the book announces her intention of one day being a novelist. Throughout she presents herself, ostensibly through his eyes, as overly committed to openness (she is an American), but in the end we discover she told the story through his eyes because there are episodes too painful for her to recount in the first person. It is a double 'kicker' – thank you, William Goldman. The tension the method casts like a cloud over the novel is a marvellous benefit. I'm not suggesting that the beginner can or should attempt to construct and explicate this sort of duplicitous compact with his readers – you need to establish authority on page 1 for it to work and the risk of failure is great – but the beginner should keep in mind that the block-breakers can also be positive plot- and character-improvement schemes. He can use the simpler ones immediately for a positive purpose rather than merely as block-breakers. Soon, when he is no longer a beginner, even the trickier versions, like my example here, become accessible if he is inclined to take risks.

Cynicism and sarcasm

If nothing else works, take a hard, cynical look at characters to discover their small failings and hidden shames. Even leading (generally sympathetic) characters can be enriched and rounded out by being made more human and fallible. Minor characters in extremis can be brought alive by the author treating them with brutal sarcasm but this runs close to the dangerous precipice of caricature exactly because they are minor and enjoy no counter-weight of goodwill elsewhere.

I remember whatsisname

A small block, but one which soon escalates minutes into wasted hours, is the temporary memory blackout on a character's appearance, age, etc. Don't sit there worrying about it! Keep your list of brief character descriptions beside you and refer to it instantly this happens – something else might catch your eye and suggest a whole new line of action as a bonus.

Unblocking the plot

In the schema we have been following, though we discussed the plot in a separate chapter, we have all along been aware that it has no autonomous existence, being a mere summary of a sequential combination of events to illustrate the theme or concept or idea of the novel. However, during the writing of the novel (as distinct from its conception and planning) plot-ting difficulties do arise. Most are irritating and tedious but not difficult to overcome. The most common occurrence actually results only from the highest standard of work in character-ization and, for some, may be a window to opportunity rather than a problem.

Characters in conflict with the plot

From holding it axiomatic that characters will be created before the plot and that frictions between characters will advance the plot, it follows that conflict between plot and character should never arise.

But this position does sometimes arise, most often when, some way into the writing of the book, the interactions of the characters suggest to the writer another plot in which the grass might be greener or even a complete new theme to be illustrated by the same characters. I discussed this with two other writers, who both said they would first finish the worked-out plot, by which stage the attraction of the alternative would have faded. If it hadn't, they would write the second draft around the new concept/plot. When I insisted that, since the interaction of the characters had led me to the choice and I would therefore not have to discard any pages, I would divert my novel to the new concept/plot, one said, 'Yes, but you're by nature a gambler and we're not. How do you know that, to extend your own analogy, these new-direction sparks between your characters aren't awakening a Frankenstein's monster?' I don't and you won't but there is more to it than mere personality differences. When this happens, I find myself utterly incapable of sticking to the old plot until I have investigated the new – and I've never yet been mauled by the monster and had to scrap the new version and return to finishing the old plot. To some it might be a block, to others an opportunity.

Links

All other plot difficulties may be generalized as 'link-problems'.

The most obvious example is a character acting in a way the reader considers out of character because the behaviour has not been motivated by what we have learnt of the character in the prior action. Or, the same problem seen from a different angle, the writer knows where he wants to arrive but has no idea how to make his characters take him there.

If the links are missing, the plot fails.

Rather than bemoaning this mishap as a failure of imagination, it is more productive for the aspirant professional to view such problems with furthering his plot as a failure to extract the maximum contribution from each character as well as the maximum of inter-character friction – that is, a shortfall in a learnable skill and therefore remediable.

As these difficulties appear during the writing of the first draft rather than at any planning stage, they are best solved by 'writing them out' rather than by extended cerebration. It is, however, prudent to check first that you have in fact completed the preliminary planning stages to the best of your growing ability and, in particular, what growth there has been in the characters in the pages you wrote before you hit the snag. Character development might suggest further interaction between the characters which could unlock your plot-block without any artifice. If not, here are some useful tools:

Skip the problem for now

Generally, there are other sections you can write, and what happens in them may well – in my experience always will – suggest motivations and actions to be established in the section giving you trouble. But let me stress that the only sections you should postpone temporarily are those where you meet technical difficulties relating to the plot and character development. Most emphatically, you should not skip sections merely because of some personal, emotional reason, because you are frightened to write them, because the material will cause you distress, because you fear you will fail with it, etc., ad nauseam. I have seen bullfighters come straight from their hospital bed to the ring; I myself went directly from hospital to the starting grid long after I ceased to drive for money; it is common cause between bullfighters and racing drivers that the man who postpones his return by a single day after he is fit is finished forever. There is no reason the same principle should not apply to writers: what you postpone today out of fear you may never return to. Irving Wallace writes most illuminatingly on the author's emotional and other hells in *The Writing of One Novel*, a book every professional writer should read.

Though the beginner should stick strictly to the proven rule above until he is confident enough in his craft to break it without stunting his future growth, there are additional solutions available to the advanced writer who has served his apprenticeship. In the novel described under role reversal above, I chose that method among other reasons because I did not want to have to write another horrid rape scene. The key word is 'another'; I've not shirked violence and other emotive issues when no superior solution was available at my level of skill at the time I had to handle them. But the main reason was not my reluctance to handle the issue, it was that the alternative presentation was superior in focussing on the reaction of the chief character to the event. Thus the story is not about the assault on the secondary character, but what the main character felt and did about it. As we have seen, that solution offered additional advantages available to me precisely because I had done my apprenticeship the hard way. I don't want to sound pompous or smug, but writing is one of those professions where the subsequent failures of those who take shortcuts early in their careers can easily be publicly measured. That applies to the thriller, which by definition deals with moral issues all decent people take a stand on, even more than to most other kinds of literature.

Write the finale first
This is an extreme form of skipping the problem but many writers find it helpful to know exactly where they want to arrive; this certainly saves writing a lot of scenes that will later be cut as unnecessary.

Cut and shut
Is it likely that your difficulty arises from having imperfectly considered how the events in the scene will further the action? When I run into a scene which seems dull even in the writing or impossible to proceed with, I write on a separate piece of paper the purpose of the event(s) in it and surprisingly often find motivations already established in previous scenes or obviously more suited to servicing by later events still to be written. The scene is dull to write because the subconscious mind already knows it is irrelevant. A very illuminating question is, 'How much rewriting will I have to do to how many other scenes if I eliminate this one?' If the answer is, 'Not much, to only a few,' you don't need to proceed with the troublesome scene.

180° turns

A complete about-turn can sometimes salvage triumph from disaster. Suppose you have a dull section – but cannot cut it because that would entail stretching the credulity of the reader too elastically by making other events and scenes carry too great a burden of motivation and information. First and foremost, look to the main character in the difficult section: is he fully realized? Is he perhaps dull because you have forced the hero's moral outlook on him? Can you tell the story more closely from his viewpoint as if he is utterly in the right?

Secondly, does a closer look at his new character not suggest some action that might enliven both the writing and the reading of the section?

Thirdly, what would happen if you briefly had him act against character? Nobody is good or bad right through: we all have sides that catch the light and we all have black corners.

Now try the same questions on the lesser characters in the section.

One my of happiest minor inventions is a stiff and correct Swiss banker whom I allowed to pop into the toy shop Detsky Mir (in Dzerzhinsky Square opposite KGB headquarters in Moscow) while waiting for the arch traitor Philby. This single soft focus on a hard man not only made him human, a child-lover, but fixed him in the reader's mind, through a couple of hundred pages in which he did not appear, until it was time to bring him on stage again. The toy shop detail was an afterthought, because I thought the section desperately dull...

Saves from the unexpected

Sometimes you will find yourself bored writing an event because the characters in it are too consistent and therefore boring, sometimes simply because the events have a predictability you have observed ad nauseam in life or other writers' books. In either case, now is the time to re-examine the quirks and inconsistencies of the characters involved in the scene for something that will give the action a hitherto unpredictable turn.

The statistician's nightmare

If you can't find anything in the characters or don't want to use what you can find (say because it would interfere with good stuff already written), it may suddenly dawn on you that the world is a random place in which unpredictable events happen. Raymond Chandler trenchantly advised the stalled writer to have someone come through the door with a gun in his hand. That's still good advice but put your mind to the variations. Be careful that even unpredictable action is relevant to the story and try not to let it sink to the level of coincidence, because that destroys your reader's faith in your ability to control the plot.

Absolutes belong to pathology

If, after trying many times, you cannot make your scene convey the exact point listed in your notes, the reason is commonly not that the point is too subtle, but that it is too rigid. This difficulty is signalled when the interplay between two moral opposites result in something that reads like Tom Sharpe rather than anything you intended. What happens is that your characters, who are after all only human, naturally see shades of grey but become caricatures if you attempt to force them into blinkered black and white postures. I often feel sorry for those serious writers, deadly intent on reforming the world, whose novels stand stiff, unconvincing and sometimes ludicrous for lack of the modest wit to give their characters a questioning edge, a little shifty evasion before the hard choices of life prior to regaining their courage, even as easily written and appealing a character trait as a little gentle, leavening irony. No day goes by but I see or hear something amusing, so why shouldn't characters in books? We will not share the character's passion unless we identify with him, and that we cannot do if he is offensively self-righteous. In addition, if we cannot sympathize with his motivation, the plot links will fail and the perceptive writer, anticipating failure, will have difficulty writing the section.

If, by now, you have concluded that the so-called plot blocks result mostly from inefficiencies in character realization, you have taken an important step towards professionalism. As soon as you realize that the plot's links depend solely on the motivations of the characters, you can respond automatically to plot blocks by looking beyond the physical hold-up to the characters, saving a deal of woe and wasted time by not being tempted to consider the plot as a thing in its own right.

Unblocking the writer

A writer, by definition, writes. But let's not delude ourselves it is easy. Because the professional writer cannot wait upon the luxury of inspiration, writing is hard work and, of all the functions a writer performs (planning, research), probably the hardest, especially for the novelist who knows at the first blank page that he must write perhaps three hundred pages more, a huge undertaking. No wonder then that writers have developed real and psychosomatic defence mechanisms to protect themselves from the terrible fear of that first blank page, and the barely smaller fear of starting on another blank page each day. Evasion can take many forms, from not appearing at your desk at all to one writer's compulsion for absolutely spearpointed pencils which consume at least an hour in sharpening each morning. But, regardless of the faintly pathetic air of such ruses, the fear is real. It comes as no great surprise to psychologists that the occupational hazard of the writer is alcoholism – rather than loneliness, as some macho writers pretend. I can't hold your hand every day at writing-time but I can give you some hints on minimizing the fear and building your confidence.

A room of one's own

From the beginning, you should set aside a room to write in. If that is not possible, the minimum is a desk permanently and solely devoted to your writing in a corner of some room. Yes, I know the legend of Thomas Wolfe writing his novels on the refrigerator and Jack Kerouac sitting on the toilet writing away in the midst of riotous parties, but Wolfe had to be rewritten by his editor and Kerouac's fame is solely the result of the manipulations of his claque.

A room or corner devoted to writing is an inducement actually to write at the set time and a reproach if you slack. You will also be surprised to find how quickly the paper mountain builds up, not only your fiction and its research, but correspondence, subsidiary files for ideas and outlines and notes, all of which need to be kept close to hand in some kind of order. In a year or two you might have three projects in circulation, all with their own space requirements. The kitchen table is far too fraught with interruptions and accidents for such valuable papers.

The importance of routine

It is impossible to stress the importance of a settled routine too much. A professional writer *writes regularly*. Choose your own time but keep to it. If you commute by train, perhaps you write on the train every morning – then don't skip any mornings to talk to fellow passengers or read the paper. John Braine advises the aspirant writer with a full-time job that three two-hour sessions per week, resulting in an output of 350 words per session, is enough. I mention this, even though I disagree strongly, because I admire his work and know that he is successful in both the literary and commercial senses. I think you should write every day, even if only for an hour, while you have another job; and five or six or seven days a week for at least six hours a day when you are a full-time writer. Nothing establishes routine like routine.

Aspirants sometimes ask if I follow my own advice; professionals don't ask but count my books instead. No, I don't. I work ten to sixteen hours a day, seven days a week. But, having piled up the pages, I feel no guilt about taking a day off to walk the hills, or two hours to cycle the lanes around my home in the Irish countryside, or a week to go to a chamber music festival once a year. The thing is that I never stop writing. I write reviews of the music at the festival, which at least pays for the holiday. I write about my hobbies, which generates much more income than they cost. When I don't have an idea for a thriller, I write about my professions, as in this book and my books on graphic design. When I can think of absolutely nothing else to write, I write letters or call local and international papers or my syndication service and ask if they have a feature or a review or a guest column for me to write. What has that to do with being a thriller writer? Most importantly, it keeps up the *routine of writing*, and in explaining to beginners the intricacies of my hobbies or work or some assigned journalistic subject, some of them very technical, I learn to communicate simply and straightforwardly. These are in themselves not small advantages. And when the time comes to write another thriller, I do not have to learn to type all over again, nor do I sit searching for the precise word, because all that practice, forty years of it since I was thirteen, just flows right on without any perceptible break. But that is where I have arrived by following good practice and building on it. Let's backtrack to where, like you, I started out.

Count your words!

Set yourself a realistic but fixed quota for each writing session, in the form, 'I will write x hours or until I have y words, whichever comes later.' Extra words you write in that time are then a bonus. Mr Braine insists that professional writers count words and he is utterly right. And I mean actual, written words individually counted, not some notional average per line multiplied by the number of lines. (This is very different from the word count you do for the publisher, which assumes that all lines are complete, and all sheets are full – i.e. no allowance is made for short lines, paragraph ends, chapter ends, lines dropped to start new chapters, part-title pages, etc. – so that you merely multiply the average number of words in, say, fifty *full* lines by the number of lines per *full* sheet by the total number of sheets.) Your own word count therefore carries no special inducement to create short lines of dialogue merely because that would make you seem so much more productive.

How much should you write each day?

That depends on which stage of your novel you are at, your circumstances and some extraneous factors. I agree with Messrs Hemingway, Goldman and Braine that first drafts should be written to completion at the greatest possible speed in the minimum time; you can then spend as much time as you like on the polished version as long as that, too, progresses at a steady rate, which will normally slow down a little towards the end of the novel as you pay special attention to drawing all the strands together neatly. Arthur Hailey, on the other hand, each day writes, rewrites several times and then polishes perhaps 600 words as a final draft, but this is more a pointer to Hailey's great experience as a journalist than to a model the novice novelist from any other background should emulate. I aim for 3000–4000 words of rough draft per day which allows ample time in a nominally ten-hour working day to read and correct the day's output (literals, awkward phrasing, deletion of repetition), answer correspondence, do the computer's housekeeping (copying discs, etc.). I used to write thirteen days out of every fourteen and spend half the fourteenth at the library, but what with the Oxford Reference Shelf on my computer and the Internet a punch of the button away, I now work seven days a week. This doesn't mean I never take a break, merely that my computer is portable and battery-operated so that whenever I wish I can work on the beach or in the back of a car or in the dull passages of the film I'm watching with my family.

3000–4000 words of first draft per day is a level first achieved after more than a decade of constant application as a full-time novelist, and it still seems to me a good target, though I manage better when things go really well. You should *start* with a much more modest target (say an *average* of 175 words per hour) and every month adjust it upwards by an increment of 25 until you reach your natural best speed. If it is of interest, I think 800 words an hour of rough first draft is an upper limit but I should certainly not like to have the rewriting problems of an author who works at such incredible speed.

On second and third drafts I do (on a computer so that there is almost no physical retyping) 200–300 words an hour if the going is good and much less if it is not. It is impossible for me to suggest a firm target for your second and third drafts because so many variables personal to you will have to be considered: a steady flow at about 50–75% of the speed of the first draft is the best I can honestly say. The important thing is not speed but never to break the flow by missing a writing session for any reason.

Earlier I mentioned that my most recent novel of 130,000 words took only 18 days to completion of the first draft. That is exceptional. Two further drafts took three months with a couple of breaks, which is approximately 50% of the rate at which the first draft was written. The implication is that with practice your first drafts may become much quicker, but rewriting will always have a certain minimum time requirement.

Still more routines
Finish what you start. Never leave a novel half-finished even if it is obvious it will be a real stinker. You might learn much even from a stinker but, more important, you will gain the confidence

of a truly huge task completed. If you stop halfway, you may never have the confidence to start again.

Accept no excuses from yourself. Writers are inventive people. Shortly after becoming a writer, I took up smoking a pipe. Time-lapse photography of me at my desk showed that during one eleven hour day I spent just over an hour filling, tamping, lighting, relighting, knocking out, scraping, cleaning my pipe. It was a sub-conscious defence mechanism. I stopped smoking and cut my workday to ten hours of total concentration and immediately became more productive. Now that my child is at university, my working hours have crept up again, but the routine has taken hold so that I manage to get much more work done.

Start work *immediately* at the given time on any day. If you postpone work one day, the next there will be even more reasons to delay. Don't let it start because, within the week, you will be doing no writing at all.

Don't daydream about the riches your writing will earn you. It won't. At best, if you don't fritter away your time daydreaming, you will be able to earn a living at something generally more enjoyable than whatever you do now – or at least once you're over the hurdle of writing the first words!

Set a date to start writing your next novel and *start* on that day, regardless of whether planning is finished, regardless of the enticing vistas of research you now see spreading invitingly before you if only you could spend another week at it. No excuses!

Thinking time

We've talked much about flashes of insight, of the stillness that overcomes the writer just before the idea takes hold of him. This applies not only to the planning stages of the novel but to sudden insights you will enjoy during its creation if only you give yourself a chance. For either purpose, it is essential that you have time to think quietly; I do my thinking walking or cycling four or five miles in the Irish lanes or the Adelaide Hills every day. This is time apart from and in addition to your writing time, on which it must not be allowed to encroach. An hour or two a day should suffice. One writer with a perfectly regular bowel movement sits on the toilet for an hour every morning because that is her 'thinking time' and the only place in the house where the children dare not intrude. When you're planning or researching a novel, more of your time should be given over to this 'thinking time'.

A mantra

Idle hands create no masterpieces, so put your hands on the keyboard of your computer immediately and start typing. If nothing else comes to mind in sixty seconds, type 'The quick brown fox jumps over the lazy dog.' Type it over and over again until something comes to mind, as it soon will. The quick brown fox is a wonderful guardian against daydreams and other tricks that the writer's mind plays on him; the mind will soon settle, as if deciding that the terrors of the blank screen cannot be all that great when they are soothed by something as small as a quick brown fox. Don't break the spell by pausing to delete the quick brown foxes, carry on writing what comes into your mind; you can lose the quick brown foxes later.

That one helps for the first blank screen. There are other mantras that help for the first blank screen, or for that matter any blank screen you may have to face first thing in the morning or afternoon or evening:

'In the dawn

'None of us will ever forget how

'The next day the madness started when

'Not one of them believed me when

'Of course it had always been possible that

'It really was very difficult to understand why

'Out of nowhere

'To this day the whereabouts of

'Where, oh where

'I still wonder whose fault it was that

'If the gods had been with

By now you probably have the idea and can make up your own list of all-purpose starter phrases. Write them on a sheet of paper and stick them on the wall in front of you and use them in strict rotation without favouritism. The idea is to complete the sentence using the name of one of your characters and that will, we hope, suggest a second sentence to you and so on until the invention flows smoothly. The starter phrases themselves end up on the cutting room floor in the editing because they are hackneyed and have served their purpose.

A variation of this technique is to stop writing at the end of each session in the middle of a sentence so that you have something to be going on with the next day.

Reading

I don't know any authors who don't like reading but books are the devil's candy and it is too easy to claim some book is essential to your work simply because you would *like* to read it. When you are engaged in the actual writing of a novel, as distinct from planning and researching it, put off *all* reading until after you have achieved your day's quota of words. Many authors prefer not to read other people's fiction while engaged in a novel of their own for fear of influences creeping in unannounced and unnoticed. When I am writing a novel, I read non-fiction unrelated to any current hobby for fear that if I read about my hobbies something interesting will distract me.

The lesser of two evils

Nothing motivates and disciplines the writer so much as poverty. I spend whatever I earn, partly to keep that fine edge of ambition honed by imminent hunger. But to be fair, I had years of living on the knife edges of advertising, motor racing and film making to practise a certain poise. Don't give up your job to write full-time unless you have at least two novels accepted for publication and a third nearly finished.

9. The Power and the Pain: cutting and rewriting

Good novels are not written, they are rewritten. Great novels are diamonds mined from layered rewrites. The same applies to thrillers but even more so because, in addition to the intensification of insight into characters brought on by rewrites, rewriting can sharpen up the pace astoundingly.

When to rewrite

While writing your first draft (or second in the John Braine method), resist the temptation to re-read what you have written merely to pat yourself on the back. When you have the complete draft to hand, that's the time to rewrite. First, correct all literals (typing errors) and delete repetitions while reading through quickly for sense. Now do your cutting and rewriting (the rest of this chapter is devoted to the procedures), then *put your manuscript away for at least six months* before hauling it out for final reading and, if necessary, polishing or even another total rewrite before offering it to a publisher. Nothing sharpens critical faculties like the distance of time.

Cutting

There is little point in reading and rewriting anything until you have a complete draft because that wastes a lot of time on sections you might later cut in total.

Begin by looking at your novel through a telescope rather than a microscope; you'll get down to miniatures soon enough. The procedure is the same whether you are rewriting a first draft or cutting a big novel to some commercially viable size.

The power and the pain: cutting and rewriting

Books and parts

First, can you cut whole books or parts from one part-title to the next part-title without doing any damage to the rest? Another way of looking at my novel *Festival* is that it always was a thriller, hidden by four times as much guff about the arts in Australia, and that I cut 80% of the first draft to be left with my small, tight thriller set against the arts. So, what happens to your novel's direction when you cut a book or part or several parts completely? In various combinations?

Chapters and sections

Next, can you cut whole chapters or sections from break to break without damaging the whole? Are there subsidiary characters who require sub-plots only for their own purposes, or characters who appear only in sub-plots? Is the sub-plot essential? If the character goes, 'his' chapters and sections can all go, too. Or, if the character is essential, will removal of sub-plots relating *only* to him hurt or perhaps even improve the main tale?

When reducing *Eight Days in Washington* to the length the publisher thought commercially viable, I first cut all the chapters relating to the history and background of the female lead, then all the chapters describing her motive for murder. This was not the end of my cutting but it accounted for three-fifths of its volume and took a tenth of the time the other two-fifths consumed. It also strengthened my book immensely as a thriller – before it had been a novel rather lacking in tension because the reader knew from the first page who the murderer was; in the cut version the mystery and tension are maintained until the very last page because the unravelling of the motive now becomes a tense sub-plot in its own right. Another way of looking at it is that the motive was presented three times in the original, once through the eyes of the murderer, once through the eyes of the victims, once unravelled by the detective, of which only the last survives.

Still on whole chapters and sections, ask yourself if any were written, or sub-plots introduced, merely to show off your expertise about technical matters or esoteric places. Unless setting and expertise is relevant to essential action which forwards the plot, readers will know it for padding even if it delights jaded editors. Again, you will be able to cut chapters or sections from break to break. Be ruthless rather than lenient with yourself – if any expertise or description is obviously required, you and your editor will both be able to spot its absence. If you go in for pyrotechnics, the critics will burn you, and the techno freaks are not well enough defined as a market to make it commercially safe to defy the general ban on technical exhibitionism. If you can't resist the temptation, switch to writing sci-fi.

Historico-literary, craft and commercial reasons for not indulging in expansive descriptive settings we have covered elsewhere. Here the pace of your narrative should be stressed: long static descriptions slow the reader down irritatingly.

If you have many sections or chapters of equal length, especially where they alternately offer opposing viewpoints, and it looks a little mechanical, this is often a signal that one half of them should go, that you've bent too far to be fair to all your characters and that you should now plump for one side or the other. Simple, accidental mechanical rhythm should be broken up by reshuffling but only after you have assured yourself that amputation is not a superior remedy.

Pages and paragraphs
If there are no further pieces that you can cut from break to break, look for the longest units you can cut within sections, several pages or paragraphs at a time. Here you should look with particular suspicion at static descriptions (again!), long expository passages either descriptive or in frictionless dialogue (if you can't cut them, mark them for rewriting into action), repetition in different form of what you've already told the reader, telling the reader what he should already know from general knowledge, characters that can be either cut or merged into other characters for better effect and economy of effort by the reader, and once more anything that is a drag on the pace of your tale.

Sentences
Penultimately, cut any sentences that meet the qualifications stated above. Then cut any sentences that seem to you awkward or which you have difficulty rewriting. You will be surprised how many sentences can be cut by this test without doing the narrative any harm – they seem to signal their uselessness by their inability to make sense when read aloud. Another kind of

sentence that can go is the one which merely keeps the dialogue going ('And what did he say then?'); longish speeches are an accepted convention of the novel and, anyway, you're not writing for idiots.

Superfluous words

Finally, getting down to the real nitty-gritty, every word must work for its living and work hard. Superfluous words are easy to spot: the sentence flows better and makes a stronger impact without them. Adjectives should be the first to go, but don't be too brutal with the adverbs unless there is more than one of them to the same verb. Superfluous words are also found in any phrase that can be replaced by a single word.

Yet more cuts

Rewriting will itself suggest more cuts by giving you a different slant on the material. But, before you start rewriting, you should try the wily craftsman's trick of rearranging the material you have left because a new combination might suggest further cuts to you, as well as new possibilities.

Originally, I intended presenting *Reverse Negative* as the leading character's diary in chronological order with, bound into the novel (diary) at the date he received them, all the computer synopses, recounting the activities of everyone else, in a single fan-fold section.*

However, many people who read the book in manuscript told me it was atrociously hard sorting out who's who and on which side at what time. That this was a valid complaint was borne out by the fact that, after I made it much easier by sorting the synopses separately into chronological place and by providing a list of dramatis personae, at least one well-regarded critic still thought I was maliciously setting intellectual traps for him. Distributing those sections of the story supposed to be synthesized by the computer to their separate chronological places in the narrative not only made it easier for readers to follow the

---

* Some of my publishers were actually prepared to support the expense of this mad scheme but I now doubt many libraries would have bought a book so easily damaged.

story but added substantially to the tension because the forward action was now shared between all the characters rather than being narrated by one, and the reader couldn't tell who was the good guy and who the bad until two-thirds through the novel. All this advantage was gained despite the fact that the rearrangement made possible cuts of a fifth the previous wordage.

A mistake or learning to choose better?

Before we move on, it is necessary to say something about your attitude to material being cut or rewritten, as distinct from your attitude to cutting and rewriting as a routine function of creating a novel. Don't view material you will cut as a mistake made in an earlier version. See the new, leaner version instead as a superior choice among many. The right attitude will help save you from the hubris that wrecks the books of those whom much publication has made arrogant. Your work will be improved by stringent vigilance until the very last book you write. The example above is from a very early book. Yet, more than twenty novels and over thirty books later, I recently had a similar experience.

After a draft, and two full rewrites, it occurred to me that the first chapter of the thriller was superfluous. It showed the chief character on a routine, if portentous, day at the office. Don't misunderstand me: there was nothing wrong with the chapter in itself. The character did fascinating work in an interesting industry; the information presented was crucial to the rest of the story. As an opening, the chapter would not lose me any sales or readers. It was good stuff. But after a while I saw that it wasn't good enough, that there was a superior choice. The chapter as a whole could not be moved anywhere else; it was chonologically impossible without making it blatantly obvious to readers that I shuffled chapters artificially to put a bigger bang in the front of my book, a definite no-no, for no-one except another magician really wants to see through the magician's tricks. That the *information* in the chapter was good and necessary to the story was proved by the fact that virtually every paragraph in the chapter had to be moved elsewhere; only a few linking sections were available for cutting. One must not scorn even the smallest tightening cut, of course, but the advantage conferred by the substantial additional work was far-reaching:

the story now opened with the bigger bang of the previously 'second' chapter. The impact left my first reader 'breathless'. That's a big jump from merely being interested in someone else's work and environment, wouldn't you say? But the larger point is that if I were inclined to view material that has to be cut, rewritten or moved as a mistake rather than a choice which can be improved upon, I might have decided that because the chapter was good and necessary it was also good enough where it was, and not have written the better book that was awaiting release within the good one. Good is not necessily good enough! Good Enough is the mortal enemy of the Best.

If you are still having trouble murdering your darlings, then it is time to practise on someone else's book in order to harden your heart. See Appendix 2 for an example.

Cuts after rewriting

More cuts and rearrangements, as in the example immediately above, will occur to you if, after putting the cut and rewritten novel aside for a good long time, you read it again critically. Apply the principles in this chapter even more rigorously and you're certain to find something you can polish out.

Surprisingly often, the perspective of time infuriatingly highlights an irrelevant, if often lovable, character who somehow escaped the torch, the sword and the scalpel – but read carefully and very critically indeed, for by now he will be so well integrated as to be almost invisible. At this stage it is tempting to let him be because you don't want to rework an entire manuscript yet again. Don't succumb: ten years from now you will read the book and know it would have been great if only you had gone all the way with it... An Important Writer, the worse for drink, once dismissed criticisms of some of his prize-winning books with, 'They don't matter, I was working my way up,' before stunning me and everyone else with the statement that the one book of his that everyone present thought a masterpiece was, in his eyes, flawed because his publisher insisted there wasn't time for him to write out a superfluous character. Re-reading that novel, I instantly saw what he meant and, when I became a novelist myself, I understood his anguish twenty years after publication. Take heed, take care, cold print will judge you until the end of time.

Rewriting

Writing your first draft, you should write only to please your-self because freshness and enthusiasm do not grow well in the compost of ulterior motives.

Your ideal reader

In rewriting, however, it helps speed many decisions if you carry in mind some ideal reader. We have seen that women make up a very large part of the book market, but what I have not men-tioned yet is that only about two per cent of the population at large are regular readers. Book readers are therefore an élite and may be assumed to be intelligent. (They also used to be distinctly middle-class but I doubt that is true in the age of tax-subsidised library membership and relatively cheap paperbacks.)

Even more important is the fact that, rather than watch the entertainment on television which requires no effort and no commitment from the viewer, the book reader has sought out *your* book and is committing time and mental effort to it. This obviously marks the reader out as someone who possesses an imagination and is eager to exercise it. It may signal a hunger for greater subtlety than the boobtoob provides; I certainly assume this of my ideal reader. You can think this ideal reader through for yourself but, however you define him, you should recognize the unspoken contract which obliges you to satisfy that unique need which drives him to your book. Writers can-not exist without readers.

Once you have 'your' reader firmly fixed in your mind, test your rewriting decisions and directions against his tastes and preferences. For instance, a piece of writing in your manuscript which appeals enormously to you-the-writer because you admire its elegant phrasing will, in another writer's book, irritate the hell out of you because it is a self-indulgent irrelevance; wouldn't it then also irritate your ideal reader?

Getting your ideal reader wrong
The ideal reader is only a device to force an exterior viewpoint on yourself while your raw material is not yet in a state fit for you to seek independent outside opinion (discussed later). But,

if you're going to get your ideal reader wrong, aim for standards higher than average rather than lower because the thriller market moves upwards all the time.

My ideal reader for *Reverse Negative* (as for most of my books) was the well-educated and highly intelligent middle-class professional who doesn't mind having his mind stretched a little of an evening. Several friends, mainly academics, labelled the manuscript as 'for the upper intelligentsia only', so we conducted a test to determine exactly where the book's potential lay. Seventy-five self-confessed fiction readers were selected as demographically representative of over five hundred we found in libraries and at paperback book stands. The seventy-five were divided into three equal groups: my own target group of middle-class professionals (lawyers, doctors, upper-level civil servants and so on), a group of the intelligentsia (mainly university teachers with postgraduate degrees), plus a control group of 'other readers' (housewives, primary school teachers, nurses, office workers, 80% of this sub-sample without a university degree) whose presence would tell us if the hypotheses being tested – the book's appeal to the intelligentsia or the middle classes – were totally off beam. The test consisted of giving each person two-thirds of the novel to the point where all the clues are present and the deductions begin, and to ask them, 'Whodunnit?'

Well, I was proved wrong – but so were my friends. The intelligentsia bombed miserably by scoring 12%; the middle-class professionals did better but still wretchedly with 20%; and, staggering everyone involved, the control group of 'other readers' hit 64%. It turned out, on analyzing the answers to the other questions relating to the respondents' backgrounds and activities and correlating them with the test results, that 'intelligence' had nothing to do with the control group's triumph but reading habits a great deal. The academics (a skewed sample because, remember, they had to admit reading fiction before they were included) read only minimal amounts of fiction, the middle classes read a good deal more fiction, but our 'other readers' really had the habit.

And the habit, even if it was exclusively Mills & Boon (our test sample wasn't limited to thriller readers), induced a useful familiarity with and acceptance of the conventions of fiction, which in turn led to greater ease in coping with those abstruse variations and ultra-subtle shifts which defeated the so-called better minds.

Yet over half the hundred-odd major reviews around the world mentioned the complexity of the plot in a manner which suggested only the select few would ever plumb it; at least one review (by an academic moonlighting on the *Yorkshire Post*) was hostile because of it. All the same, the book sold very well indeed, thank you, and my ideal reader is still a person who would be offended if I insulted his intelligence by writing down; you can't aim too high.

The power of suggestion

If your readers are presumed intelligent and both able and willing to exercise their imagination, this should encourage you towards subtlety rather than bluntness, towards suggestion rather than straightforward explication, and towards the insightful rather than the exterior gloss. By way of example, it is instructive to compare Ian Fleming's James Bond with Charles McCarry's Paul Christopher, both Cold War spies, both appreciative of the finer things in life – but in, oh! such different ways.

What to rewrite

Eventually, you will rewrite everything, but the process is smoother and easier if you have a structured, disciplined approach. My method is probably no better than one you might work out for yourself, provided you work it out completely, and that you stick to it and don't go wandering off into the interesting byways which will open up all the time.

- First, rewrite all passages where static description needs to be transposed into action.
- Second, rewrite all passages and sections which need alteration because of cuts.
- Third, write whatever new passages or sections need to be created because of the cuts. There should be notes on the printed copy of the manuscript about these, made at the time you decided the cut. It is probably best to write the new section without referring to the cut parts; follow your original notes instead.

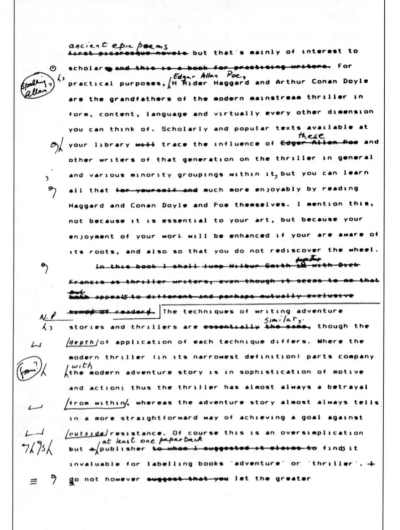

A third-draft page from the first chapter of this book – I do not always work so tidily! Note that, even on a late draft, substantial cuts can still be made.

- Fourth, rewrite all sections where the characterization needs strengthening.

- Fifth, tackle all sections where the action needs strengthening.

- Sixth, re-read to check that all the character motivation is in place and consistent, and that consequently the plot flows without hiccups. To this point, all the rewriting is done in accordance with the guidelines and suggestions laid down in the previous chapters.

- Seventh, check one last time if there isn't a little something else you can cut or move to increase pace and tension.

- Eighth, edit the whole ms line by line for clarity, simplicity, brevity, sense, persuasion and conviction. This is the toughest rewriting assignment, the line-by-line rewriting, and we shall spend the rest of the chapter on it.

The real rewrite

Even before the line-by-line re-write, you may very well have what is called a 'publishable novel'. This does not mean it *will* be published, merely that a publisher can discern within its still-rough surface the structure of a saleable novel – and may thus be willing to offer on it subject to certain developmental work being successfully completed.

However, because of the way publishing is structured, unless you have a substantial track record, you cannot reach the publisher to ask him to make this decision. And those who possess substantial track records achieved them by never showing unfinished work, by always going the last mile – and then some.

The line-by-line rewrite is your insurance, by adding the extra touch of professionalism, that your novel passes the hurdles of publishers' readers and editors to reach the shortlist of novels discussed with the publisher (and perhaps read by him) prior to an offer being made or a dialogue being opened with you.

When should you print?

One of the disadvantages of the computer, in so many other ways a boon to writers, is that in the very process of creation it destroys the tracks of the act of creation. If there is no audit trail of the wrong path taken, retraced and corrected, little is learned. The smooth, glossy finish on the computer's screen and printer output can not only be misleading, but can hide processes that may be advantageous for you to consider consciously.

Imagine for the moment that you work on a typewriter, rather than a computer. Now, even before the line-by-line, you will have lots of sheets of paper in pretty tacky condition. Because it is on paper, there is an audit trail of creative decisions. The all-important development work has not been plastered over. Further development work to ensure publication rests on a visible foundation.

It is therfore important at some point to make a print-out and *to work on it* for at least one complete cycle of the rewriting process, rather than merely to print the finished manuscript out for the first time when it is ready for offering. Remember, agents and editors and readers read words on paper, not on screen. Sheets of paper in your hand give you an opportunity to see your thriller *from their viewpoint*.

Later you will make up your own mind which stage is most beneficial for you to work out on paper, but for those of you who will print out only one working stage, I suggest that it be the line-by-line.

Mechanics

You now have another bite at the cherry, another chance to weigh each word and phrase. To make maximum use of the opportunity, reformat to a different width before you start work either on paper or on screen because even this can give you a new perspective on text whose familiarity may tend to set the words in concrete. Precisely because on a computer, unlike a typewriter, you will not be retyping *all* the words, consider each word, phrase and sentence extra cynically.

Actionwrite

The most important advice I can give you is to seek out and select the strongest, most active words you can find, to write in the active rather than the passive voice, and to bend over backwards to find ways to prune still further.

There are at least three things wrong with this sentence:
'*I was going to let him have the box when I am dead.*'
Try this instead:

'*I intended bequeathing him the box.*'
The second version is strong where the first is flatulent.

He was sleeping soundly.
is slack against
He slept soundly.

While doing your line-by-line rewrite, check that all sections have hooks (Chapter 5) at both beginning and end. Amend as required.

If a picture tells ten thousand words, a line of dialogue is at least ten times more communicative to a reader than a line of descriptive text: If

He urgently wanted a grappling iron.
  is weak and
He grabbed for the grappling iron.
  is both more active and specific, then
'*Pass me that grappling iron, quick, man!*' he shouted.
  is not only stronger in itself, but more likely to involve the reader in the action because it builds tension.

Use dialogue to break long descriptive passages; lone mountaineers and single-handed ocean-racing yachtsmen speak to themselves.

Pace

By this stage, the sole difficulty with the pace of your novel, if any, should be a technical one. This happens when, in the rewriting, you unintentionally create a chopped-salami cycle and countercycle of action and counteraction (or reaction) of roughly equal lengths with a repetitive rhythm. You probably won't find out about it until after you have finished the rewrite and then you will despair. Don't. I've never yet failed to fix this apparent disaster by a spot of reshuffling and page renumbering.

But you can, in the line-by-line rewrite, add immensely to the tension and pace of even an already good novel. At the most basic level, you should pace your sentences. There is no harm in long sentences in description but in action rhythms should shorten with the breath of the man performing the action. '*Do you carry a firearm?*' is a drawing-room question, while '*A gun! D'you have a gun?*' is more likely to be uttered by a man attacked. (This particular solecism was pointed out to me from the manuscript of *The Zaharoff Commission* by the outstanding Australian free-lance editor Shirley Young.) Also, towards the end of the book, long sentences requiring more thought might irritate readers already tense for the climax – or even spoil the climax because they march to a different drummer than the action. Split such sentences or, even better, delete half of each altogether.

Vocabulary

Should you use 'big words' or should you stick to the basic 800 words philologists say everyone recognizes? Neither. You should use *precise* words. Remember your ideal reader; I bet he has a thesaurus and a dictionary – and so should you. You should also have *A Dictionary of Modern English Usage* by H. W. Fowler and *The Complete Plain Words* by Sir Ernest Gowers. However, where two words will convey the same meaning, use the simpler one. Remember, the story's the thing, so don't complicate or obscure it with pompous writing. Check how simply the leading thriller writers express themselves and the amount of information and emotion they convey by virtue of precision: they aim single shots at the bull's eye rather than spraying words scattershot in the hope of eliciting some reaction.

A final check

Run your novel through the spellchecker of your word processor. Add the names of the characters to its custom dictionary to be certain you rendered their names consistently.

Now check the whole thing again, line by line. I call this the meta-check, because I consider it a sort of metaphysical double-check of *meanings* one can sometimes overlook while engaged in nitty-gritty mechanics, all of which will by now be absent. You are now reading your novel not as a writer but as a hyper-critical reader cursed with an ultra-literal mind.

- Does every sentence convey your meaning as clearly as possible? Is it also as simply constructed and phrased as is possible? Len Deighton aims for 'the sentence readers may think they can write themselves' which sounds easy until you try to write such a sentence without sacrificing any information.

- Does every sentence convey the maximum amount of information in the least number of words? Brevity for its own sake is not an aim here as the length of each sentence depends on your purpose – but every word must count.

- Does every sentence convey *only* the sense you wish it to transmit without irrelevant undercurrents (jargon: sub-texts)?

- Is every sentence likely to have the effect on the reader that you desire – will it persuade the reader?

- Does every sentence carry the stamp of your conviction and commitment to the extent that you will never be bored with it or ashamed of it?

If you have meticulously attended to all these facets of each sentence, you will by now have an instantly recognizable style of your own.

Congratulations, your novel is ready to send to a publisher. Or perhaps you prefer to proceed cautiously and get some outside opinions first on whether it needs more work.

Professional help before you approach a publisher

Publishing is no longer a profession for gentlemen. It is a business, pure and simple. Editors cannot afford the time to teach you to write or even, in most cases, to guide you in the finishing touches that would make a promising manuscript publishable. It's yes or no, in or out. It follows that the novel you offer must be as good as possible to persuade a publisher to make an offer or at least to open a dialogue by telling you exactly what is wrong with it, which implies an invitation to offer it again when you've rewritten it. Obviously, you want to avoid the situation where you get one shot at the bull and, no matter that you miss by a fraction, never another chance. Agents (next chapter) are in many cases now the first hurdle you must vault on the road to publication, but their time and patience are as limited as that of editors, in most cases more so since they work on commission rather than for salaries.

It is therefore intelligent to obtain some reader reactions and, if possible, hints for further cutting and rewriting, all of which can improve your manuscript still further before you offer it.

Family and friends

There is much professional help available outside publishing houses and the offices of literary agents. First of all, ask any of your relatives *who are regular thriller readers* to read your final manuscript (don't offer them any intervening draft because that will confuse the issue) and let them tell you what they think about it, which characters they liked, if the climax surprised them, etc. Next try your friends who are regular thriller readers.

Exceptional friends

It is useful if you have among your friends a civil servant of the old school, devoted to precision of language. I offered Stuart Jay, once a senior civil servant and then General Manager of the South Australian Film Corporation, a manuscript copy of *Reverse Negative*, hoping for no more than a general opinion (there was no chance his film company would buy the story), and he stayed up nights pencilling over my language so that he shares the credit for the many critics and readers who were impressed with the 'gentle, precise, dry wit'.

New writers may think editors are supposed to provide this kind of service to their authors but they haven't time and those who, at great sacrifice to their leisure, make the time are likely to be failed writers who want to rewrite *your* book rather than merely excoriate the shortcomings of your language. I was so incensed at an American editor who, without comment, sent me seventy sheets typed with his own hands on his own typewriter as cancel sheets – jargon for replacements – for a novel of mine 'for approval', that my agent had to restrain me physically from stuffing the man's advance in his orifices. Andrew McCoy, faced with a similar situation, had a David O. Selznick rubber stamp made: 'Editorial alterations signed but not read by Mr McCoy', stamped each offending page with it, and returned the lot – and the editor was thick-skinned enough to go ahead and publish his own altered version!

You must have friends or know people who are well educated and are widely read. I don't remember anyone ever refusing to read and comment on a manuscript of mine; most people are flattered to be asked. You will soon find out which people are useful to your novel and which are too diffident or inarticulate to give you anything worthwhile. My friend, the financier Kerry Harvey, would, for instance, give me an overnight general opinion on any manuscript of mine because he is an insomniac and a voracious reader but, if there were financial shenanigans described, I knew I could ask him to read the new version after rewriting to accommodate his comments, if necessary repeatedly until it was right. Another friend (whose husband doesn't want her name mentioned!) is good for general hard-hitting critique on sex scenes and specific information on perversions. If you have enough friends or acquaintances willing to help, you can ask each to pay special attention to a particular aspect by saying, as you hand over the ms, something like, 'Listen, you worked in government for a long time. Of course I'd love to hear your general comments about the story but would you look out in particular for any place I went wrong with the civil servants and politicians.'

Advance editorial advice

Next step up this ladder, is there some way you can obtain advice from professional editors before you show your ms to the editor at any publishing house that is likely to publish it? First, don't send your manuscript to me or any other writer. If you get any response at all, it will be a placebo. When I was a student, a professional, published novelist wrote me a letter saying: 'You will never be a writer. Try something less demanding like accounting.' My books have long since sold better than his and are better reviewed, too. When I was struggling to be published, a professional, published writer wrote me: 'Your accursed fecundity has bolted with you. *Reverse Negative* is unsalvageable and unpublishable.' He has published one novel in the intervening thirty years, I've published twenty, including the book he damned. With such lessons before me I am most certainly not about to tell any other writer his work is rubbish only to find myself exposed as a fool (or, worse, envious or frightened of competition). John Braine relates the story of a writer who sent him an unsolicited manuscript and then was very angry when Braine advised him to turn a sub-plot into the main tale and dump the rest, which was affected and unconvincing; after that Mr Braine sent out placebos, too. It is no good another writer telling you only what, if anything, he likes about your work – what you want is someone telling you with relentless honesty what is wrong with it.

But there are professionals who can help you. First, try the books editor of your local newspaper. Will he either read your ms or pass it to one of his regular reviewers (you may have to pay a small fee)?

Next, which of your friends knows a publisher or editor? My financier friend Kerry Harvey's accountant's brother knew an editor, Peter Hutton, at the non-fiction house IPC, and my ms was handed down this chain and came back with a letter of detailed judgements and advice on alterations plus a list of publishers I should offer the ms to when rewritten; Mr Hutton also offered an introduction to the most likely one. Next, after the rewrite, I found Penny Kazimierczak had been at college with an editor at another publishing house; Penny Vigar obtained and copied to me a professional reader's report, which told me in detail why her house would not publish the novel. Remember, editors work not only at book publishers but for newspapers and in film and tv companies as well. When I started writing in Adelaide, I received a lot of help from the script editors and staff writers at the South Australian Film Corporation (in those days on an informal basis but now they run courses for script-writers). Crawford Productions, then a production company of tv serials, sent a senior editor who was himself an established writer to my home town to scout local talent and I used my morning with him to get a detailed critique of several mss and outlines of mine he had seen. Don't neglect any channel. My own experience with producers and directors of stage plays is that they have little comprehension of mixed narrative formats (i.e. novels) but you may do better with those accessible to you; there is no intrinsic reason why stage directors should be less useful than film or television people.

If you live in a small or provincial town – in book publishing terms anywhere but New York or London – try your indigenous publishers. At the very least, they'll tell you who would be most likely to publish your novel. Next try the local offices of far-away or foreign publishers and see if they offer any advice on either the narrative or its marketing. They can only say no, at worst it can cost you postage and, at best... An editor at a local house told me to try Anne Godden and Al Knight who were then still at Thomas Nelson in Melbourne; they could not publish me there (Nelson's publish no fiction) but gave me introductions in London and New York, helped me find publishers and agents and, when they set up on their own as Hyland House, invited me to publish with them. Obviously, my 'local' editor knew Anne and Al intended going into business for themselves and were looking for likely authors...

If you can find out who the local publishers use to report on fiction, you can hire the same readers. The fees are usually not very high. Don't tell them you're the author – make a new title page with a pseudonym – or you could receive nothing but flattery.

Exceptional editors
If you have been published even once, further opportunities open for your second book. There are a few exceptional editors who will take immense trouble without going too far and they are worth seeking out if, unusually, you have a choice. My good relationship with my Australian publishers has permitted me on several occasions to request that they have my ms edited by the freelance Shirley Young who is not only a demon on precise vocabulary and exact meanings but alert even to such minute points as the writer deviating momentarily from his normally preferred style of punctuation. She, like Stuart Jay, is also extraordinarily well-read and informed, which is not true of many editors, especially at publishing houses big enough for editors to 'specialize'.

Editors who are successful, rather than failed, writers can also be exceptionally advantageous to work with. After I complained to one publisher about the quality of the 'editing' perpetrated on my novel, he hired the distinguished novelist Andrew Taylor to do the job right. The work was so outstanding, I asked who had done it. Ever since, I have, where I could, asked that Mr Taylor be brought in to handle my ms, both fiction and non-fiction. It really does help to have an editor who is culturally in tune with the writer; many of the modern conglomerate editors know more about market research than about literature.

I trust I have persuaded you that a good book is always the result of team work! But putting the right team together takes time and effort, and you must start from where you have already arrived. And, as this section has, I hope, demonstrated, having been published before does not guarantee that the in-house 'editing' of your book will be of a high standard or release you from the duty of care to the children of your own talent.

Free advice is best

The old maxim that free advice is worth what you pay for it doesn't apply to the unpublished author, as we have seen above. In the list so far, the only advice that costs is that of second choices: reviewers rather than editors, editors' readers rather than editors.

There are people who will give you a professional opinion for money. Many agents charge a so-called 'reading fee' to consider whether they will offer your manuscript; give them a miss. Other agents charge the same fee but will give you a written report if they decide not to offer your manuscript to a publisher. Whether this is worthwhile depends on the fee; my own opinion is that anything up to four figure sums is too much for what I can get gratis elsewhere. Certainly, my agents, when they are any good, offer editorial advice and suggestions free of charge to *publishable authors* who have taken every conceivable step to present the best manuscript they can.

There are also people who will edit, rewrite and improve your novel but their main prey is the media personality with a marketable name and too much vanity to hire a ghost-writer. Such auxiliaries charge realistic (read profitable) fees for their services and I can't imagine any real writer using them.

Rewards come last

By now you should be in no doubt as to why professional writers insist that a real writer writes for show and rewrites for the money. If you want to be published and become a professional, all this work is absolutely necessary. But, now that you have finished it, you can seek an agent or a publisher for your thriller – and know that you are giving yourself absolutely the best possible chance of publication.

10. Now Barabbas was a Publisher

Let me immediately apologize to those for whom parts of this chapter will come as a disillusionment and a shock. But my purpose is to help you be published so I can borrow your books from my library or buy them in paperback, and enjoy reading them. And that won't happen unless you take a realistic approach to the *business* of getting published.

Let's get the worst over with first

When you set out to find a publisher for your novel, you enter a strange and wonderful new country called 'Infotainment'. It used to be called 'the Media' and had a near-autonomous division called 'Publishing' of which the publishing of books was a sub-division, within which novel-publishing was a niche containing a great many educated and charming men and women who cared about literature, who would care about you and your book, who would nurture you from a fledgeling until the day you became either a bestseller or *The Times Literary Supplement* gave you the accolade of a full-page review or even both, and the New York *Times* on the same day hailed you as a genius. That is the world of publishing I entered twenty-five years ago as a professional novelist; it was wonderful but, let's be crystal clear, it is of no more than nostalgic interest to you.

If you want to be a professional novelist, for a start disabuse yourself of the comforting notion that any of that survives, or that the traditional patches of old-style publishing which manages to hang on by its fingernails will survive much beyond the turn of the millennium.

Flux

In the last quarter of the twentieth century, publishing, the profession you now intend to join with your book as your entry-ticket, underwent greater change than at any other time since Gutenberg invented printing. These are only the highlights of the greatest relevance to authors:

- Instead of many hundreds of publishers of varying sizes and interests, there are now perhaps twenty large *entertainment* (not just book publishing) conglomerates which own between them all the significant mainstream publishing houses – and whose sole interest is profit.

- Instead of an author joining a publishing house, he presently links his fate with an editor and moves with that editor from publisher to publisher.

- Instead of the agent being merely a conduit to the editor and a financial adviser who distanced a pair of good friends, editor and author, from any possibility of financial acrimony, the agent has become a powerful entity in his own right through increasingly having sole access to many publishers.

- Instead of competing to present the largest variety of themes, publishers now compete to grab the maximum shelf space with the currently fashionable theme, which as I write this (1999) is books about lawyers.

- Instead of books being more important than the other media, the balance of power has shifted to where books are on the verge of becoming an adjunct to the visual media.

Infotainment is a huge and powerful country in which you should not travel without a map. It is constantly in upheaval from earthquakes, so your map should be periodically updated. It is a professional function for you to update your map yourself. Your survival depends on it.

A rosy future?

These are the changes I expect to affect the second half of my career as a professional novelist, and which will affect the first half of your career equally:

- Editors, of whom many are already functionally illiterate, will become out and out dealmakers, product managers 'creating' books for their employers in exactly the same manner that a product manager in a soap company draws together available resources and talents to create a new soap to fit a marketing trend.

- More and more publishers will refuse to read unsolicited manuscripts. Access to the executive with 'yes-power' will for the beginning author and even the old hand be closed, as it has been in films for a generation or more.

- A concentration of editorial and financial resources on 'big' books instead of variety will close opportunities at the bottom of the market. (In this regard, thank your lucky stars you are a *thriller* writer, operating in a very big market, because the larger the market the more openings there are at all levels.) Books which appeal to smaller but still financially viable readerships will stand less of a chance.

- The literary agent will become the most important personage in publishing for the author, because the agent alone will have access to editors. That makes the author's literary representative, a commission agent, the arbiter of what sort of book is published. That is both a symptom and the result of a fundamental publishing shift from literary criteria to commercial ones.

- Many or even most books will primarily be judged on their suitability for translation to the visual media, with a view to selling film, television and multimedia rights to the sister companies in the conglomerate which owns the book publisher.

The future always arrives
However, there is an upside to all this:

- If your book fits the marketing fashion of the moment, skill requirements which historically applied when the merit criteria were literary will be lowered.

- As one path of access to publishing closes, another opens. The Internet, for instance, opens near-costless avenues to publication which before either did not exist or were very expensive or otherwise unwise.

- As a corollary, self-publishing has already become more respectable – see the next chapter.

- The rewards for the successful will be immense.

- Since writers will no longer be tied to publishers or editors but to agents, books will not be sold to publishers for a running average advance somewhat below their market price, as was the rule before. Instead agents will sell each book for the going price to the highest bidder, which often fetches an advance beyond the economic viability of the book, regardless of who published the author before.

- Though the number of novels published in any year is stalled at the turn of the millennia as the new mega-publishers 'rationalize' everything in sight, I expect that numbers will soon start to creep up again proportionally to the increased wealth of readers, as in times past.

- Within this 'rationalized growth', the more popular genres, including the thriller, will benefit disproportionately simply because the mindset of big business is to reinforce success.

- Those who are published will benefit from much more professional promotion and distribution because at that no-one can better the big multi-nationals, certainly not the lovable but amateurish publishers of a nearly bygone age.

Flex
What can you do about all this? Certainly, since the huge industry you want to enter, the ninth largest in the world, is in flux, you must remain flexible.

Among other things, that means that you must not overlook any avenue through which you can market your novel.

And equally certainly, you must take a professionally business-like rather than an artistic view of marketing your novel.

Given that your book is good as literature, and thrills as a thriller should, being published becomes a matter of getting through the door and, once inside, persuading someone that you have a solution to one or more of his problems.

Once you have grasped that, finding a publisher for your book becomes much easier.

Selling a book and its author

Finding a publisher for your novel is not an event but a process. It is even misleading to speak of finding a publisher for 'a novel' in the singular because most publishers dislike one-shot ventures; the process is one of finding a publisher for your novels, plural. While the first novel lies in a drawer awaiting polishing or rewriting, you should write another, and so on. Editors and agents interested in your work will be keen to hear you are already working on a second or even third novel, so that their investment of time and money in you as the author can be spread over several books rather than having to be recouped on a singleton.

The literary agent

Right, you've now exhausted all the initial sources of advice about how to improve even your final draft and you are keen, nay, impatient to offer it to the proper, correct publisher. An agent would know the best publisher, because it is his business to do so. In many cases – and an increasing number of them – an agent is the only one who can present the book because the publisher won't accept unsolicited manuscripts from anyone else.

Until quite recently, many agents would not take on an author until he had at least one book accepted. Because of the change in attitude of publishers towards reading unsolicited manuscripts, that position has now changed quite drastically. Many agents are now very keen indeed to see first novels, and some specialize in it as a way of building up their business quickly. Agents have seen, as I have and have described above, that in future authors will 'belong' to the agent, as they are now tied to editors and move from publisher to publisher with 'their' editor, and before that stayed with a single publisher for a very long time or often for an entire career. Agents with foresight are positioning themselves to turn their new-found power into income. This is to the advantage of new authors.

Authors tend to stay with good agents, as with good editors, a very long time, and to move with them to new agencies or publishing houses when they move. Thus I followed David Stewart Hull, my agent at the New York office of Curtis Brown, when he set up on his own, with the blessing of the head of the firm, James Oliver Brown, whom I liked and respected. I followed Nick Austin, my London paperback editor, to four different publishing houses in fifteen years. The tedium and opportunity cost of finding a good agent or editor are too great to lose touch with the one who is right for you.

Twenty years later, however, many agents tend to specialize, so even these bonds are weakening. I now have two agents for technical books, one in New York and one in California, a different literary agent in California to deal with film makers and also with publishers on lead novels, and shortly I shall have to find a new London agent after a dozen years of handling my own affairs there (or more precisely, after having my attention focussed across the Atlantic in that time), because I have a novel I want to sell first in Britain as its setting is primarily British. Note that one can select an agent for a specific purpose. The bigger and livelier agents have their own contacts with specialist agents and use them as sub-agents; for many, perhaps most authors, having one competent agent handle all their books and affairs in this manner may be perfectly adequate.

There is a group of agents who demand, as proof of your talent, publication in the 'little magazines'. Since these correctly pejoratively named journals don't pay, and the short form is utterly unrelated to the novel, never mind that the literary criteria of the little magazines are twee and unworldly, that's stupid. Give such agents a miss: they are trying to pass the buck of a responsibility – that of literary judgement – which they claim to perform and are paid by part of your income to perform. Agents who insist that you have at least one book sold before you hire them live in yesterday's cloud cuckoo land; you can do better for yourself than they can.

Agents receive 10–15% of gross income. If an agent tries to charge more, go somewhere else. If sub-agents are used, the commission usually rises to a total of 15–25% but is worth it because this usually concerns income *additional* to the primary, main sale.

You need no contract with an agent but do write him a letter confirming the commission rate and make the point that, if you do leave him, all the books on your account go with you without further notice. This is necessary because some agents may argue that, if they sell a book, they are entitled to a continuing cut of the royalties. If they are no longer performing services for you, this is clearly rubbish but, more to the point, can cause trouble when you want to take a book in which an agent claims a residual interest away from one publisher and give it to another. There should be no grey areas in everyone's understanding of this agreement.

You should limit your approaches to agents (source lists below) to those who represent thrillers or even prefer thrillers or specialize in them. Most will handle thrillers because it is a huge market they cannot afford to miss out on, so there is no point wasting your time with agents who aren't really interested or specialize in another field. Some references give a list of authors represented by agents. You may feel either that an agent for the writers you like to read will have special enthusiasm for your work, or that he may be wary of taking on a competing author. I take the first view; if your book is publishable, it will not be a carbon copy of anyone else's style, and the editors such an agent regularly deals with on the whole are likely either to specialize or to believe that synergy of similar books is better marketing than scattershot variety.

You approach an agent in precisely the same manner as a publisher, so we'll deal with that below after discussing how you choose a publisher to approach.

Choosing your publisher

You will find publishers listed in the same places as agents, in yearbooks for writers. For London and the English-speaking world outside the United States, try *Writers' & Artists' Yearbook*, published annually by A & C Black of London (publishers of this book); for New York and the States try *Literary Market Place*, published biennially by R. R. Bowker of New York, or the latest edition of either *Writers' Handbook*, published by The Writer of Boston, or *Novel & Short Story Writer's Market*, published by Writer's Digest Books of Cincinnati.

All you want at this stage is a list of those publishers who accept fiction or, better still, if they specify it, your kind of fiction: thrillers, adventure stories, detective tales. Now visit your library with this list in your hand and check who published the books you most enjoyed reading – we're still working on the assumption that you write what you enjoy reading. Mark those publishers either on your list or directly in the reference book. Next, ask the librarian to let you see the lists of forthcoming books from all the publishers. In Britain, *The Bookseller* conveniently divides the forthcoming books into categories, so that you can see immediately which publishers are most active in your category. You stand a better chance with a publisher with an active list than one who publishes only a few novels a year.

Your shortlist should now have about ten publishers on it. Next, consult the advertisements in *The Bookseller* or the publishers' most recent lists to find out which proportion of each publisher's output is made up of thrillers. Rank your shortlist in order of the percentage of their output allocated to thrillers (small publishers will long since have been eliminated because they publish only a few thrillers). Most of the larger publishers have imprints that are mainly thrillers, and editors with managerial and financial clout to run them: these names will naturally gravitate to the top of your list and you can arrange them in the order in which you like the same kind of books as they like, a pleasing symmetry. The purpose is in the first instance to address yourself to an editor who devotes himself either fully or at least substantially to thrillers and is therefore knowledgeable and keen because, if he can't find enough publishable thrillers, his job will disappear.

Submitting your ms

Decide if you will try to find an agent or submit directly to such publishers as accept unsoliticited manuscripts. Both can be time-consuming and costly in postage. While it is still possible to sell a book directly to a publisher, my opinion is that you may as well get an agent and get used to the new dispensation.

Now ascertain from your author's yearbook which publishers on your list accept complete unsolicited mss, which prefer sample chapters with a synopsis, and which request a preliminary letter.

Those which prefer or insist on submissions through an agent should not appear on your list at all, no matter how well you think your thriller will suit their list. If they're so lukewarm that they 'prefer' no unsolicited manuscripts, they may give your unsolicited submission to a junior clerical skivvy, one of which I saw painting her nails at a major publisher while she stared with cowlike incomprehension at someone's life's work. In three years, as an avid consumer in her own time of Harlequin books, she discovered several romances which were publishable – but unfortunately her firm publishes no romances – and passed up probably at least ten times that many decent thrillers, which her firm does publish. In her own words, I was 'the first important person ever to speak to' her. Her job was literally to hold faith with a senior executive's rash public statement: 'We read all manuscripts.' It is the decision-making power of the reading 'we' that matters. Don't waste your time on people who don't want to hear from you.

Agents have similar rules and preferences to publishers, listed in the same reference books.

Follow their rules scrupulously in offering the ms, with the exceptions noted under the next sub-heading.

Some publishers and many agents will accept query letters by e-mail, which can speed up the process. A very few agents will accept queries by phone but I would advise you, unless you are a professional salesman or have other professional verbal presentation skills, to write a letter instead. You might think from the writing here that I may be a glib fellow, and from the rest of my career that from a lifetime of making presentations, and selling ideas to publishers over lunch, I could sell an idea on the phone to anyone. Not so. A publisher who takes you to lunch is predisposed to believe you, and you probably have a track record with him already. A publisher or agent called cold is professionally sceptical and you cannot be certain of his full attention. To those who do not know me, I fluff more calls than I do well. I prefer to write to them, and give them time to let my idea build in their minds, rather than risk an instant and final 'No' on the phone. In any event, the only 'Yes' you are ever likely to hear will be instantly qualified by, 'Write me a letter about it.'

Do not telephone those who insist on a letter.

The query letter

Your first letter should very briefly tell something about you, and outline your book in a paragraph or two. One page is best, two pages is barely acceptable, three pages are too many.

Among the personal details it is *essential* to include all of these if true: professional training or experience relevant to the story of your thriller, other experience relevant to the story of your thriller, any publication whatsoever even if non-fiction or technical or otherwise apparently irrelevant to a thriller, and the fact that you are working on a second or a third book already. These are all items of information extraneous to the book that you can trade on as an author, and which may give the decision just that tilt in your favour if there is doubt.

Furthermore, if your book is based on a true story which received major publicity, you should mention that prominently.

It is easy for writers to overlook 'any publication whatsoever even if non-fiction or technical or otherwise apparently irrelevant' or even to find it faintly embarrassing. Yet I received a commission for a most profitable book from a book packager who had seen my Internet site and decided I sounded like the man he wanted to write a book he had been dreaming about for years, and another commission for a television thriller serial from a producer who read my syndicated classical music column in his local paper and from there my books in his library... It really doesn't matter what you have written, it is the simple fact of publication which reinforces the judgement of the editor or agent, who is trying hard to find a reason to take you on. Give them all the help you can to say, 'Yes!'

The synopsis

For the contents of the synopsis, refer to Chapter 5 on plot or follow the rules you learned at school and college for the making of a précis or summary. Briefly, the shorter the synopsis, the better, given only that it *demonstrates the complete chain of motivation for the key actions of all the major characters*. The purpose is to leave no reasonable question unanswered. The art of the synopsis for either the written book offered for publication or the unwritten book offered for commissioning is a very large subject covered for all aspirant and professional writers (not just thriller writers) in my *Writing Proposals & Synopses That Sell* (David St John Thomas, Publisher/*Writers News* Library of Writing), which also addresses the selection of sample chapters for maximum impact.

The 2000-word outline made prior to the second draft in the

John Braine method is such a closed-chain synopsis, and can be further cut down to 2–3pp, single spaced, for the synopsis. However, the synopsis you send to a publisher or agent is a selling document, rather than strictly a literary chain-of-evidence, so be certain your enthusiasm shines through.

Even a complete manuscript should be accompanied by a synopsis no longer than a single-spaced page to tell editors what the novel is about – they may not want that sort of thing at all and will remember the courtesy when next they see your name on another ms. In fact, I don't supply a synopsis in the strict sense; instead, I write the blurb for the dustjacket front flap and half-title page but from an unpublished author this could seem pretentious.

Iteration

When all the publishers and agents on your shortlist have rejected the ms or declined to represent you, go through the same procedure with the second ten, and then the next ten and the next. When the ms has been rejected by every likely publisher and agent, rewrite it into different form, retitle it and start at the top again: I sold *Reverse Negative* the forty-fourth time it was offered in London to a publisher who had twice before rejected it. Jerzy Kosinski's novel *Cockpit* was rejected by one editor in the same publishing house where another editor had already contracted for it! It may not be a fair world for writers, but some of its irrationalities are to the writer's advantage.

Submissions and exceptions

Writers' yearbooks tell you all about double-spaced typing or printing on A4 paper, etc., and warn you not to make simultaneous submissions. Double-spacing is right, the rest is nonsense. A4 paper is a disaster in New York because it is too big for the boxes agents commonly use to protect manuscripts in their peregrinations up and down Fifth Avenue. Any good stationer stocks the American standard size (8.5 x 11 inches) or will cut a ream for you; it is also a standard computer paper size.

Many publishers and agents have an embargo on dot matrix printing. If you use a computer, get a good printer – inkjets are cheap if you cannot afford a laser printer – or use the one at the office or a printing service. Most publishers and agents will not accept computer discs in lieu of hard copy and none will accept whole manuscripts by e-mail.

As for simultaneous submissions, this is the book publishers' association chancing its arm. When offering material to magazines and newspapers, multiple submissions are not made because there is a presumption that you will accept their standard rate of pay and because they will often use the piece without referring to you again, merely sending you a cheque. But a book publisher does not go ahead and publish your novel: he makes an offer you can accept or reject. The practical effect of heeding this advice about not making multiple submissions is that it puts the publisher who has your manuscript into a monopoly position as there are no competitive offers for you to consider. And he would know immediately if you try to better his offer at another publisher as there would probably be a delay of at least six weeks in your reply to him while you waited for a response from the second publisher. Publishers have no right to demand single submissions and there is no obligation on you to help them destroy a free market. Don't tell any publisher you're making a simultaneous submission. Three or four copies in circulation to either publishers or agents should be enough.

Don't forget to enclose return postage with your ms or query letter. International reply coupons will do for a query letter but are expensive for manuscripts; instead send bank notes in the publisher's local currency obtained from your bank's foreign currency department.

Foreign places and editors

Don't just look to your own, local publishers, especially if you live in London or New York. If you live in New York, you should try at least the publishers in London, and vice versa. Your book may be more attractive to publishers in the other place for reasons you cannot be expected to know. On the back of the title page in books you will find the country of first publication so, if all those you like were first published in a foreign country, add their foreign publishers to your list (you discover the publishers' names from *Books in Print* for that country, available at your library). This costs a lot in postage and the return postage you must always include, but it certainly paid off for me. Preliminary letters of enquiry can cut down on postage expended.

Or get an agent in that country. At least this will cut down on postage and he will have better knowledge of local conditions and personalities than you can be expected to command.

If a substantial part of your novel is set in some exotic part of the world, you could also approach the regional publishers. Canada, Australia and South Africa are very big markets for English-language books and, especially if you have settings there, the local publishers may be interested. Editors in the far-flung branch offices of publishers with headquarters in London and New York sometimes have their own budgets and publications schedules, and are often very helpful with editorial advice if approached right.

Building a pre-natal relationship

If you immediately receive an offer from a publisher or an agent agrees to represent you, congratulations. But most of us collect multiple rejection slips. Don't let them hurt you – you should by now have a second novel 'in the drawer' and be working on a third to keep your mind off disappointment. Don't cross a publisher or agent off your list for your next book just because he sends you a cold rejection card or form letter; you need him more than he needs you.

What you're hoping for, failing publication or representation, is a dialogue in which the editor or agent tells you why he is rejecting your novel and perhaps advises you what to do with it. Take heed, this is professional advice you can't buy for any money. First, and most obvious, you are no longer dealing with some faceless 'Editorial Director' or 'Editor-in-Chief' but with a person who will go to bat for your novel with a decision maker or a committee as soon as he is convinced that your novel will enhance rather than damage his reputation for editorial or marketing acumen. Rewrite it according to his suggestions and offer it to him again, or to any other house he has suggested by name. Mention his name in your letter to the next publisher or agent – these recommendations are not lightly given and are as good as an introduction – but don't be so gauche as to include a copy of his letter.

Write the man a note of thanks – keep it brief – and ask if he wants to see your second novel while you fix the first one. Some editors and agents, seeing from your original letter that you are writing a second novel (always include this information), will promptly advise you to put the first in a deep drawer, lock it and throw the key away – and then ask to see the second novel. Don't get your back up! Instead, celebrate, because you're on your way to publication.

It is true that many first novels are so bad that they should be burnt; my own very first effort lay for years in a locked drawer until one of my publishers discovered a hole in her schedule, remembered this piece of crud and absolutely insisted that her need was greater than my pride and didn't I like money? The best review said it 'out-Hollywoods Hollywood'; fortunately the publisher and I had retained just enough sense to stick a pseudonym on it and could so blush in private. The notorious over-preciousness of first novels is one very good reason to tell an editor or agent you're busy on a second or even third novel, because that is more convincing than telling him straight up you're a professional entertainer who goes out nightly to do your act, not an arty-farty (an editorial pejorative worth noting both for its vehemence and its precision) waiting to be patted on the back for your single effort.

Once you have an editor hooked, don't lean on him and try to hurry publication. I was in correspondence with John Blackwell for nearly five years before Secker made their first offer for one of my books; then, all of a sudden, they bought one, then a couple more that were in various stages of completion, then commissioned seven novels from me over the next seven years before I left them.

An agent will not have that much patience. But there are more agents than publishers now, so you can view whatever you do get out of any agent as a learning experience.

Until an editor or agent says, 'Yes,' the prudent author will keep building up a relationship with any other editor or agent who offers him dialogue.

Then, one day, and the day always comes to those who work hard enough, an agent or an editor says, 'Yes!' – and your life becomes your business.

11. The Pro: a writer's business is his life

When a publisher says yes, don't give him your soul out of gratitude; he's not doing you any favours. You may have to take whatever advance he offers or a small increase over his first offer, or an agent may increase the offer substantially by threatening to take the manuscript, already declared publishable, to another publisher. The advantage to the author of a large advance is not just the cash, pleasant as it may be, but that a large advance forces the publisher to invest time and money in promoting the thriller to recoup his investment.

Read your first contract carefully even if you have an agent to look after its details; it is unprofessional not to understand what you sign.

Your first contract

Many contracts conform to a set, reasonable pattern. There is a simple but adequate sample contract in Appendix 1 and various writers' associations have their own model contracts available on request. The option clause (i.e. that you offer your next work to the publisher) is virtually unenforceable and I refuse to sign it, telling publishers instead to rely on my commercial good sense to publish with them again unless they prove incompetent at marketing my books. If you leave it in, 'fair and reasonable terms' for your next book is acceptable, 'the same terms' is not – you will want more money.

Watch the subsidiary rights. Let the hardcover publisher have the right to license the volume to a paperback house because that helps keep book prices down and, if he makes a good paperback sale, next time you can ask for a bigger advance in expectation of another; but you *must* get at least 60% of paperback income, not 50%.

By all means let the publisher handle your translation rights, unless you're with an agent who has a competent translation department. Through an agent you should usually receive 81% of the gross income from sale of foreign language rights but you have to pay for the reading copies sent out. Publishers normally give you 85% of the net income ('net' being after deduction of the foreign agent's 10%) but you don't have to pay for the copies used – swings and roundabouts.

Other volume rights, such as book club rights, are traditionally also licensed to the publisher, essentially because only publishers (and a few agents) can get through the front door of the book club merchants. This may change as agents become more powerful, so keep an ear open for trade gossip.

Publishers have no right to broadcasting licences (except straight, undramatized readings), television, dramatic, film or multimedia rights; you should retain those solely for yourself. Clauses claiming for the publisher 'any other right that may come into existence' you should strike out. If your book becomes a videogame, it won't be due to any skill of the publisher and he has no right to a share of the income.

Don't risk losing your first contract for it but add to the advance and payment clause of your second contract the words 'provided that the publisher shall advise the author of acceptance or requirements for alteration within six weeks of receipt of typescript or any alterations to it.' The phrase ensures that you get feedback on necessary rewriting while you can still remember characters, not when you've already written several books more and may have to spend weeks thinking yourself back into the earlier book before you can confidently do the alterations the editor wants. It also ensures that you get paid promptly; without the addition, you might find that a year or eighteen months can slip by before you get paid while editors 'consider their response' (editorial bull for skiving off). A minor purpose is to ensure that you can leave a slack publisher with your rights intact but without having to return the advance; I've only had to do this twice. The only exception should be those contracts on which you are paid in full on *delivery* (not approval, a different matter altogether).

Don't forget to check that a clause is included to recover your rights should the publisher sell fewer than a given number of copies in a year, let the book go out of print, go bankrupt, or fail to meet any of the undertakings of the agreement (i.e. not pay you!).

Another important clause you should check is the one committing the publisher to publish the book within a given number of months, usually twelve or eighteen; if you can't find it, add it.

You should also have the right to send auditors to check your accounts with the publisher and, if an error is found, the publishers must pay your auditors. I don't know of any financially dishonest publishers but I once found an error worth about a thousand pounds (then $2400) merely by checking my royalty statements against what I had been told about the size of the print order and then querying it with the publisher's accountant, who apologised profusely, kicked the computer and sent me a cheque.

Never forget, the publisher has not *bought* anything from you – you have merely licensed him as an agent to trade in the fruits of your mind. It is a franchise operation in which you are the principal without whom nothing proceeds.

The professional writer

Your first contract is just the beginning. It doesn't make you a professional writer. It merely puts your foot on the ladder. A writer's life is indistinguishable from his business, because so much of what he does is input to his output. Think of writing, the activity, as a vocation and this becomes easy to understand.

But a professional attitude starts before publication, and helps towards it, as we have seen. What we haven't discussed yet is how a writer educates himself and continues educating himself throughout his career.

How the writer educates himself

Next to practice at your keyboard, the books in the public library are your staunchest allies in the quest for skills. Everything else is second-best but we live in a free society and the choice is available.

Only the youngest aspirants still mention a degree in Eng Lit as a route to writing one's own novel. As preparation for a career in publishing or journalism it may make an indirect contribution but my usual advice when asked this question is to study something more directly useful for finding a job even in journalism, say politics or economics. Some of the most striking prose I have ever enjoyed was written by people in business school with me; conversely, the ranks of DLitt alumni do not include any great novelists or even any good ones that I am aware of. Many writers regret their inability to read the great Russian, French, Spanish, German, Italian and Japanese masters in the original and this is something for aspiring writers who still have their educational choices ahead of them to think on, together with the knowledge that simultaneous translators are well paid and have travel opportunities.

Some jobs offer opportunities to hone writing skills and of these I particularly recommend journalism and advertising copy-writing because of the discipline they inculcate. Incidentally, I think it probable that the aspiring novelist will obtain the best-value training from the least prestigious kind of advertising, retail advertising rather than the big agency 'image' accounts, because the pressures of both deadlines and space are so much greater. It is also said that one learns more about people on a small-town paper than on the big national confections and, even though I cannot speak from experience, I believe it to be true. There are other occupations in which one can acquire writing skills while earning a living: publishing, broadcasting, even the civil service. I learnt much about persuasion and conciseness through writing business reports while on second-ment from my advertising agency to management or staff jobs in large commercial and industrial firms.

Universities offer creative writing courses. Adult education courses for aspirant writers are offered by colleges and other further education centres. In addition there are correspondence schools offering courses of various lengths and credibility. For the aspirant unable or unwilling to make an extended commitment, foundations and other bodies run short-term intensive (often residential) courses. Obviously, the value any novice may gain varies enormously not only with the quality of the instruction but in relation to his own existing abilities and needs. Much of what these creative writing schools put out is snake-oil, but if snake-oil will help you be published, then it may be worthwhile to you. Lena Kennedy, the East End granny who became a bestselling author, says she gained enormous confidence through reading her writing to attentive members of the middle classes at her creative writing class. When you shop around among courses available to you, the test must always be: will this outlay of money and time be rewarded by publication? It is not enough merely to promise to make you a better writer – in whose judgement? One professor of creative writing in California refuses to graduate any student who has not sold a piece for publication to a commercial publisher and, consequently, in order not to have a 100% failure rate, he teaches craft and technique rather than the more attractive but utterly elusive 'art' – this is a refreshingly realistic attitude.

There is another self-education device for writers. This is the writers' circle, notably practised by the Fellowship of Australian Writers. It consists of a number of writers, published and aspirant, who meet at regular intervals to read their writings aloud and then listen to the criticism of anyone present. When the group gets too large, it splits into two groups. The important qualification is that membership is not limited to published writers (as in professional writers' trade unions and associations). In the UK and USA, such circles exist spottily on a local basis but, if your area does not have one, you can start one by advertising in a local paper for like-minded writers.

You may or may not learn something by attending writers' conferences. I find them useful for picking up trade gossip but have yet to learn anything aesthetically worthwhile.

Even if professional writers' bodies won't let you join until you are published, I don't know any which demand membership cards at the door. You can learn much about the organization of a writer's life and financial affairs by discreetly gate-crashing their meetings. Again, they are a source of trade intelligence; don't scorn gossip, it can make the difference between sending your manuscript to a keen publisher rather than one without any money for new authors. It is a commonplace that the new writer is shocked to find that established authors' sole small-talk is of money, so don't expect to learn anything of aesthetic value at such meetings.

It is perhaps worth noting that, when I first became an author, agents and publishers exclaimed at my knowledgeable approach to their business and that this respect earned me bigger initial offers that I would otherwise have had. The knowledge came from listening carefully at writers' meetings and reading every book and trade publication on publishing in the library, hardly a huge effort but one that other writers apparently scorned and still scorn. Would you travel in a strange country without a map?

That brings us right back to libraries. That's right, plural. Besides the public library, any town has other libraries: schools, colleges, universities, professional associations, private individuals, all have libraries. Learn to use a library properly and all knowledge is yours.

Finally, the full circle: a writer is not made by his education, he creates himself through his education. And, of all the tools of his self-education, none is more fruitful than honing his unique talent through unceasing practice at writing, writing, writing. Talk is cheap but a published book stands forever.

A writer's back

Many years ago my back hurt from sitting many hours on a hard chair in front of my keyboard. My doctor is part of a practice which serves a big swathe of the Carbery Coast, in Ireland's southwest. Ireland gives a tax-free existence to several kinds of creative artists, including writers, of whom many are my neighbours up and down 'the Carbery'. In the physiotherapist's room of the medical centre he sent me to there were four tables. On two of them when I arrived lay two distinguished bestselling thriller writers. One said in greeting, 'Is this the physio, or a f****** thriller writers' convention?' A bit of industrial espionage soon gained me the information that for the many successful writers who live here, back problems are prevalent well beyond statistical expectation. In fact, it became clear that successful writers suffer from back pains to such an extent that the normal illnesses of professionals of a certain age and income hardly feature at all!

If you cannot work because your back hurts too much to sit or stand in front of your keyboard, you are victimising yourself and your work by a self-induced block.

A thriller writer who wants to continue to be a thriller writer should pay serious attention to the ergonomics of his working environment, not only to protect his back but his other limbs and senses as well.

170

You should have two lights, one fairly intense as a reading or keyboard lamp, and one an overhead lamp so that the shadows are not too intense. Get the best screen you can afford, so that the characters you have to read are crisp and clear. You will be looking at them for many hours each day. I have a huge graphic designer's 21 inch screen and I work with 18pt Palatino, clearly readable from two feet away. I sit well back in my chair and read and type without strain on eyes, arms or back.

Next, consider your chair. It should have arms to rest your elbows on while you operate your keyboard. The muscles in your shoulders from which your arms hang are connected to muscles in the small of your back which are very easily inflamed. Treatment is slow and painful – it consists of kneading the sore muscles to make them worse until your body's natural defences kick in! The arms on the chair and the table holding your keyboard should be so arranged that your wrists are horizontal when you type. The chair seat should be at such a height that your feet rest comfortably flat on the floor. The chair should have lumbar support or at least a cushion in the small of your back.

I sit for one week on a chair of shaped foam and reinforced glass of my own design. You can buy similar 'ergonomic' and 'lumbar support' chairs. Every other week I sit on a Finnish kneeling chair which a local cabinet maker built and padded for me. You can buy similar chairs out of the catalogues of any office furniture supplier, and at many furniture stores. I highly recommend a kneeling chair and, for those who can afford it, alternation between back support and the natural position the kneeling chair enforces.

Your concentration will lag after fifty minutes. Do not sit at your keyboard for longer than that. Stand up every fifty minutes, make a cup of coffee, stretch, walk around the room, check the post, whatever. That will be advantageous for both your mind and your body, and thus for your work.

Take regular exercise. It is part of your work as a professional writer. That American editor who all those years ago so rudely questioned me about my health and habits had a point. Sluggish bodies envelop sluggish minds which write poorly. Swimming, brisk walking and cycling are, in order, the best exercises yet devised. Jogging may take less time for the same effect.

A professional attitude to change

We have noted several times that the thriller writer's environment of publishing is subject to violent and sometimes unpredictable change. A professional will stay on top of and take advantage of these changes. The following are merely examples of matters which will become important to you probably sooner rather than later.

Rights you haven't even heard of
The big multi-nationals who own the major publishers also own visual media and electronic media. They can see a rich future for what you and I may now consider tricks for children and computer geeks. They are already trying to take your electronic rights for the same price they pay for the book. Don't let them rip you off! If they want electronic rights, they must pay for them and show that they will exploit them within reasonable time or return them to you. In most cases film, video and multimedia subsidiary rights are worth far more than the original literary rights. Sit down firmly before you read the next sentence. Even more valuable are the merchandising and exploitation rights in popular characters. This is the sale of toys and T-shirts and whatnot, and the licensing of the names of popular characters and their images for other products. Steven Spielberg made more money out of the merchandising of Michael Crichton's dinosaurs than out of the movies... Don't carelessly sign away your rights to valuable property. If you haven't yet spent ten minutes considering that just the name James Bond is worth millions, please take a break now to think about it. Remember, no-one knows which characters or other concepts will survive to become marketable brands. Fifty years ago Ian Fleming created James Bond because he was bored on his holiday at fly-infested Goldeneye, his house in 'idyllic' Jamaica, and because he wanted the money to pay for an American car.

Cyber-publishing, or repurposing for a pension
Hypermedia, which is publication on CD-ROM and the Internet, has created a new market among non-book readers for existing literary material. In addition, multimedia applications, which you may think of as a cyber-publishing equivalent to television

or films, are adaptations into audio-visual form of literary material for information or entertainment. Finally, there already are highly portable electronic 'bookholders', soon to be common, on which people can read on screen a book delivered to them electronically via their computer at home; generally these are not yet new purpose-created books but volumes from the back catalogues of lively publishers. The infotainer's jargon for all this is 'repurposing'.

Do not scoff because the enthusiasts use awkward jargon. Gutenberg was probably ridiculed for claiming that a 'press', which everyone knew squeezed grapes so that one could make wine, was an implement for printing books. Instead, see the opportunity: it is almost tangible. The new media are bringing you a huge new market which never read books before. It may be a market which wants to read your newly minted book. It is certainly a market into which authors with a backlist can sell their old books and which will increase the income from their new books. I can quite see some elderly authors taking their entire pension from repurposing their old books into the new media.

A twenty-first century perspective on self-publishing

It used to be that self-publishing was scorned because only the rich could pay for it, thus bypassing editorial judgements of merit. Vanity publishing, in which those with more ambition than skill were flattered out of their cash by 'publishers' who weren't, was and is regarded even less favourably. In the last quarter-century, with almost anyone being able to afford it, self- and vanity publishing have become axiomatically *infra dig*, with the reason rarely spelt out. Usually the reason was simply that most vanity- and self-publishers, lacking the professional skills of real publishers, did it so badly that their efforts brought nothing but disgrace on all their kind.

That has changed with the arrival of the Internet. Vanity publishing will always, unless it becomes subject to legal regulation, in the vast majority of cases bring nothing but disgrace on both parties to it. We can therefore leave it behind us, except to note that the Internet, by making self-publishing so cheap and the exchange of information so open, will probably destroy a lot of vanity publishers, and a good thing that is too.

But genuine self-publishing is about to become not only reputable but to achieve a certain status.

The Internet is an almost costless 'printing press' insofar as electronic distribution costs only a fraction of producing a printed book. It is a distribution chain for real printed books that no shop-bound bookseller can match; Amazon, the Internet bookseller, in a couple of years became the largest bookseller in the world. But most of all, it is a marketing and promotion medium that leaves traditional mail-order and print advertising for dead. On the Internet virtually no skill is required to perform all the functions of a traditional publisher! Of course, if the book is bad, it will still die, but that is true even of bad books published by traditional publishers.

Self-publishing is already respectable in the trendiest place on earth. The California agent Ken Atchity has picked up several authors who had successfully self-published their books, sold the books to traditional publishers, and created careers for the authors. (Atchity, himself a writer on Ancient Greek culture among other things, interestingly publishes his own books with the oldest and most traditional of publishers.) The Internet merely widens the scope for self-publishing, and vastly speeds up the process of sorting the chaff from the wheat among self-publishers.

This raises the question: if self-publishing is so easy with the Internet, will the traditional publisher die out? True, the traditional 'literary' publisher is almost dead, but the added-value merchandizers of infotainment who have replaced him will always be more skilled at extracting maximum returns from a literary property than any but a tiny handful of authors who master the Internet. This question is akin to claiming that because Frederic Forsyth produced a successful film, *The Fourth Protocol*, from his own book, all writers will suddenly turn into film producers. Forsyth was a hardheaded businessman long before he ever became a thriller writer.

However, I can easily foresee a future, which is almost upon us, in which an agent will demand, instead of publication in little magazines, that a would-be client should at least have published a few good web pages or stories in web-zines. And I confidently forecast that any writer who can prove that he has sold a few thousand copies of his electronically self-published thriller by electronic delivery over the Internet will find an agent and a publisher.

The Internet has thus made self-publishing economical for competent marketers. But much more significantly, it has made self-publishing an economic tool for everyone seeking thereby to attract the attention of a professional literary agent or publisher.

Your future as a professional writer

As I said, these are only examples, but they are examples where you can take your own fate into your own hands and shape it as you will, a radically different world of opportunities from only yesterday when a publisher shaped your fate as a writer.

In this new century, in the most profound sense, you will create your own future in your own image by your own sweat, iniative and talent. We are back where we started this book, but with greater emphasis.

Remember – perseverance gets you published.

Good luck!

Appendix 1: a model contract

MEMORANDUM OF AGREEMENT

made this .... day of ....20.......

BETWEEN...

of...

....

(hereinafter called the Author) of the One Part and the Company of NAME OF PUBLISHER of ADDRESS (hereinafter called the Publishers) of the Other Part for themselves and their executors administrators assigns and successors (as the case may be) whereby it is mutually agreed as follows:

1. The Author agrees to write a work provisionally entitled   Work

....

(hereinafter referred to as the Work), which shall consist of approximately .... words.

2. The Author undertakes to deliver two (2) copies of the   Delivery Work (prepared in accordance with the publishers' *Notes for Authors and their Typists*) by the

....day of ....20.......

Should the Author fail to deliver the typescript by the prescribed date the publishers may if they think fit decline to publish the Work, in which case the Agreement will be subject to cancellation by the Publisher and any moneys paid shall be returned. If in the opinion of the Publishers any pages of the copy are unclear or unsuitable for the printer the Publishers shall be entitled to have those pages typed or legibly copied and to charge the cost of such typing or copying to the Author.

3. The Author shall at his/her own expense obtain from the owners of any material in the Work including any quotations of which the copyright is not his/her own, written permission for the use of such material.

Quotations

4. An index, if required, shall be supplied by the author at the Author's expense and sent to the Publishers at the same time as the corrected page proofs.

Index

5. The Author agrees to correct the proofs of the Work with all reasonable promptitude, to see the Work carefully through each stage of production and to bear all costs of corrections and alterations made by him/her (printer's errors excepted) exceeding ten per cent (10%) of the cost of typesetting. The Publishers shall be at liberty to set off all costs against any sums which may be due to the Author.

Proof Corrections

6. The Author hereby warrants that the Work is an original work, has not been published in volume form within the territories covered by this Agreement and is not in any way a violation of any existing copyright, that it contains nothing libellous or defamatory, that all statements contained therein purporting to be facts are to the best of the Author's knowledge and belief true, that the Author has full power to make this Agreement and will indemnify the Publishers against any loss injury or damage (including any legal costs or expenses and any compensation costs and disbursements paid by the Publishers to compromise or settle any claim) occasioned to the Publishers in consequence of any breach of this warranty or arising out of any claim alleging that the Work constitutes an infringement of copyright or contains libellous or defamatory matter. The Author further warrants that the Work contains no obscene or indecent material.

Indemnity

7. The Publishers shall, unless prevented by war, strikes, lock-outs or other circumstances beyond the Publishers' control, produce and publish the Work at their own risk and expense with reasonable promptitude. The Publishers shall have control of the entire publication. Paper, printing, binding, jacket and embellishments, the manner and extent of promotion and advertising, the number and distribution of free copies for the Press or otherwise, and the price and terms of sale of the first or any subsequent edition or impression shall be at their discretion.

Publication

8. The Author being the sole owner of the copyright of the Work grants to the Publisher during the term of unrestricted copyright the exclusive right to print and publish the Work in book form throughout the world subject only to the provisions of Clauses 9–13.

Assignment of Copyright

9. In consideration of the rights and privileges accorded to the Publishers under this Agreement the Publishers agree to make the following payments to the Author:

Payment

For the first and any subsequent impressions a fee of .... pounds (£   ) payable .... which shall cover all copies of each printing, irrespective of markets into which the copies are sold.

A royalty of .... (%) shall be additionally payable on the trade edition after the sale of .... (   ) copies of the Publisher's edition; the royalty shall be calculated on the published price on all copies sold at a discount of less than fifty per cent (50%); on copies sold at a discount of fifty per cent (50%) or over, the royalty shall be calculated on the Publishers' receipts.

On the second and subsequent impressions the royalty shall be .... (%).

10. On copies produced by the Publishers for bulk sale to an overseas publisher or overseas book club (e.g in the United States of America, Canada, Australia, New Zealand) and sold at a price inclusive of royalty, the Author shall receive ....per cent (%) of the Publishers' receipts unless such copies be the subject of Clause 9. Should such copies be sold at a price exclusive of royalty, the royalty shall be divided in the proportion of sixty per cent (60%) to the Author and forty per cent (40%) to the Publishers.

Overseas Bulk Sales

11. On copies produced by the Publishers and sold to a book club in the United Kingdom at a price inclusive of royalty the Author shall receive .... per cent (%) of the Publishers' receipts unless such copies be the subject of Clause 9. On copies sold at a price exclusive of royalty the royalty shall be divided as in Clause 10.

Book Clubs

12. The Author and Publishers shall mutually control all paperback rights in the Work and shall divide the royalties received in the proportion of fifty per cent (50%) to the Author and fifty per cent (50%) to the Publishers.

On all copies sold of a paperback edition produced by the Publishers themselves the Publishers shall pay to the Author a royalty of .... per cent (%) of the published price on all copies sold at a discount of less than fifty per cent (50%); on all copies sold at a discount of fifty per cent (50%) or over the royalty shall be .... per cent (%) of the Publishers' receipts.

13. The Publishers shall control all translation and reprint rights (including separate manufacture and publication outside the United Kigndom) in the Work, the receipts from which shall be divided in the proportion of sixty per cent (60%) to the Author and forty per cent (40%) to the Publishers. The Publishers shall also control all digest, serial, one-shot periodical, quotation, dramatic, film, microfilm, anthology, radio, television, audio and video recording rights in the Work and shall divide the net proceeds with the Author in the proportion of fifty per cent (50%) to the Author and fifty per cent (50%) to the Publishers.

14. The Author shall be entitled to six (6) free copies of the first and two (2) free copies of any subsequent impression of the Work on the day of publication and to buy further copies at trade price. The Author shall be entitled to buy, at trade price, copies of any other books in the Publishers' list.

15. The Publishers shall render the first two accounts of the Work as at 30 June and 31 December next following the date of publication and subsequently annually as at 31 December. All moneys due to the Author shall be paid within three (3) months of the said accountancy dates except that no account need be rendered, unless specially demanded, nor payment made in respect of any period in which the sum due is less than twenty-five pounds (£25), in which case the amount will be carried forward to the next accountancy date.

16. Should the Publishers at any time allow the Work to go out of print or off the market and being given six (6) calendar months' notice in writing by the Author fail to re-issue or reprint and put on the market (unless prevented by circumstances beyond their control or because the Work at that date is under revision or in the course of reproduction for re-issue) an edition of the Work, then all rights granted by the Author in respect of the Work shall revert to him/her.

Reversion

17. The Publishers shall, not less than twelve (12) months after publication, be entitled to sell surplus stock at the best price such stock will fetch. The Author shall be offered the right to purchase such stock at the estimated sale price; if the average price achieved within the royalty accounting period proves to be lower, the Author shall be entitled to an appropriate refund.

Overstocks

18. Should the Publishers go into liquidation other than voluntary liquidation this Agreement shall thereupon terminate and the Author shall be free to license any other person to print and publish the work, notwithstanding anything to the contrary contained or implied in any part of this Agreement.

Relicensing

19. The Author shall not, without the written consent of the Publishers, publish or cause to be published any abridgement or expansion or part of the Work in serial or book form, nor shall the Author prepare otherwise than for the publishers any material which shall affect prejudicially the sales of the Work.

Competing Works

20. The Author agrees to give the publishers first option on the publication of his/her next full-length work.

Option

IN WITNESS WHEREOF the Parties hereunder set their hands the day and the year first above written.

By or on behalf of the Author

Witnessed by ....

Address ....

....

.... Occupation...

For and on behalf of the Publishers	Witnessed by...............................
	Address ....
	....
....	Occupation ....

Appendix 2: a rewriting exercise

Generally speaking, exercises for writers are a waste of time. They should instead spend their time writing. But in the cutting and rewriting, the assassination of their own darlings can be so distressing until they have some experience of committing 'a few necessary murders' that an exercise may be helpful.

Any exercise will however only be helpful if it is set at a level that exercises the mind strenuously. It is no good setting as an exercise to thriller writers a well-written thriller, because it will already be too tight. Setting a badly-made thriller as a test is worse, because it is usually full of holes, which those taking the test are not qualified to fill. And if it is a trashy book published because the author is already a bestseller, you might be left with the erroneous idea that you, too, can get away with slack work.

What you want, if you want to practise on someone else's work, is a novel by a good writer on which to apply the suggestions for cutting and rewriting in Chapter 9. I suggest Gore Vidal's *Empire*. This is an excellent novel, full of historical insights, both quick and expansive character portraits, and plenty of action. It is in form an historical thriller about a disputed inheritance, with subplots about American politics.

However, in a strictly technical sense, it is in parts not all that carefully written. Perhaps Vidal is simply too important a writer for editors and copy editors to suggest changes to him. You need feel no embarrassment at the impertinence. Here is Vidal himself (p. 517 of the André Deutsch edition) on Henry James's speaking and writing style, in a sentence inserted as an aside into the middle of a James speech which runs on for many lines: 'James filled his plate without dropping so much as a single syllable of a speaking style which hardly varied now from his novels, which were, for Hay, unlike the writer himself, too long of wind for the page while delightful when accompanied by James's beautifully measured voice, far less British in its accent than that of Henry Adams, who sounded exactly like the very Englishmen who had so resolutely snubbed him and his father during the latter's ministry to St James's.' Nothing wrong with this sentence, except that it runs on too long for most modern attention spans; even on that ground it can be defended as criticism by pastiche. Note the delicious ambiguity of 'unlike the writer himself' – is it James himself whom Hay finds inoffensive or is it Vidal who does not like James all that much?

Take any ten-page section. Imagine you are the editor. The challenge is to sort out some of the awkward sentences without losing their subtleties. The qualification is important. If you lose the richness of the thought behind the language, and in particular the flashing wit, you have failed. Compare with some of Vidal's earlier writing, which is as rich in thought and wit, but more carefully crafted.

Next, consider the subject matter and framework of the story. Which questions would you raise in rewriting and cutting if this were your book or you were the editor? Can you, for instance, defend, or would you even want to defend, the entire section where we are first introduced to Mrs Delacroix and Plon? Or would you throw out these two characters as irrelevant, together with all the matters they raise, and present the summer camp of the rich in another way? Is Vidal making a social point here, or any other kind of a point? Is it valid? Is it necessary? Will any readers care?

Consider the much shorter section describing John Hay's visit to the dying Nicolay. What is its purpose? I don't know, but I would let it stand as interesting in itself, well within the discretion of a writer as experienced as Vidal. Would you? Should you, if this were a first book without any presumption of merit and consequent right to publication such as Vidal undoubtedly benefits from?

Make a list of similar structural matters. What would you do to 'correct' each one?

Index